# Holding on to Hope

# Holding on to Hope

*The Journey Beyond Darkness*

By Kathryn J. Hermes, FSP

With healing exercises by Helene Cote, PM

*auline*

BOOKS & MEDIA

Boston

Library of Congress Cataloging-in-Publication Data

Hermes, Kathryn.

  Holding on to hope : the journey beyond darkness / by Kathryn J. Hermes ; with healing exercises by Helene Cote.

     p. cm.

  ISBN 0-8198-3395-9 (pbk.)

  1. Spiritual healing. 2. Hope—Religious aspects—Christianity. 3. Consolation. 4. Healing—Religious aspects—Christianity. 5. Emotions—Religious aspects—Christianity. I. Cote, Helene, PM. II. Title.

  BT732.5.H455 2010
  234'.131--dc22

                                    2010011374

Unless otherwise noted, the Scripture quotations contained herein are from the *New Revised Standard Version Bible: Catholic Edition*, copyright © 1989, 1993, Division of Christian Education of the National Council of the Churches of Christ in the United States of America. Used by permission. All rights reserved.

Some Scripture taken from *The Message*, copyright © 1993, 1994, 1995, 1996, 2000, 2001, 2002. Used by permission of NavPress Publishing Group.

Some Scripture taken from *The Holy Bible: New International Version*, copyright © 1986 by the New York International Bible Society, used by permission of Zondervan Bible Publishers.

Some Scripture taken from *The Jerusalem Bible*, copyright © 1966 by Darton, Longman & Todd, Ltd. and Doubleday, a division of Random House, Inc. Reprinted by permission.

Some Scripture taken from *The New Jerusalem Bible*, copyright © 1985 by Darton, Longman & Todd, Ltd. and Doubleday, a division of Random House, Inc. Reprinted by permission.

Cover design by Rosana Usselmann

Cover photo © dblight / istockphoto.com

"P" and PAULINE are registered trademarks of the Daughters of St. Paul

Published by Pauline Books & Media, 50 Saint Pauls Avenue, Boston, MA 02130-3491

Printed in the U.S.A.

www.pauline.org

Pauline Books & Media is the publishing house of the Daughters of St. Paul, an international congregation of women religious serving the Church with the communications media.

1 2 3 4 5 6 7 8 9                                    14 13 12  11 10

# Contents

# Acknowledgments

To thank all the people who truly are a part of this book would be impossible. Friends, family, doctors, therapists, my community, spiritual directors, colleagues ... so many people have been a part of my journey toward healing and hope through many struggles in my life, and their influence and wisdom are reflected in these pages. Sister Helene Cote, with whom I wrote this book, was an important figure for directing my healing process and my writing in new directions. What is good is due to the part all these people have played in my life; I take responsibility for any mistakes. In particular, however, some people deserve my special gratitude, for without them this book would not have made it to press. The first is Sister Christine Salvatore Setticase, FSP. She is the primary reason this book made it to the hands of the editor on time. Her invaluable comments throughout the text pointed out flaws, which I was thankfully able to mend before publication. The following people read the manuscript a number of times. I want to thank them for their time and generosity: Sister Sharon Anne Legere,

FSP; Anna Welch; Sister Denise Cecilia Benjamin, FSP; Dora Duhaylonsod; Anthony Ruggiero; Tony Hermes; Sister Philomena Mattuzzi, FSP; and my parents, Gordon and Pat Hermes, who have always been a strong support to me. And lastly, it has been a delight to work with my editors, Sister Grace Dateno, FSP, who helped Sister Helene and me organize ourselves and concretize our book concept, and Sister Mary Lea Hill, FSP, who helped shape and polish the book.

# Introduction

I'd been there four days. I had left a stretched-too-thin ministry schedule to engage in a weeklong process of healing. Now, in a beautiful spot, in a quiet retreat house along the Atlantic shoreline in lovely Maine, I had waited four days for the healing to begin. "Not ready," my director had pronounced each day when we met. The words seemed like a death sentence as the precious minutes of the retreat ticked quickly by. I was running out of time, but I couldn't do anything more than rock in a swing on the front lawn—endlessly back and forth, my soul held in the icy grip of some inner blizzard, the spiritual icicles refusing to melt in the warmth of the retreat center's gentle seaside rhythm.

"Therapy," my director had told me earlier that year, "is a wonderful resource and gives you tools, insight, experience. But therapy can't heal you. Only God heals." Well, here I am, God, waiting. What is the magical thing called healing that I'm not ready for? Can you do something, anything to help me be another person, eliminate my problems, change my personality, erase my past, fulfill my dreams?

Those of us who have suffered depression, who have been knocked down by grief, stretched through major illness, or shattered by betrayal or failure, often look for more than survival. These realities can keep us locked in a tiny box, restricting the development of our personality, career, friendships, marriage, and spirit. Even if we've begun again to pray; engaged the assistance of a spiritual director; created a regimen of diet, exercise, and, if needed, medicine and alternative health modalities, we feel somehow there must be something more.

This book is about that something more.

Almost ten years have passed since I wrote *Surviving Depression: A Catholic Approach*. Readers have stated that what they found most helpful in the book was the connection between faith and their emotional struggles. Somehow, they knew that God was there in the midst of the chaos, but they lacked the eyes to see him and the ears to hear him. *Surviving Depression* offered tools for connecting in faith to God. For a long time I've had this nagging feeling that people needed something more than what they could find in *Surviving Depression*. They were ripe now for some deepening spiritual transformation—but the unfolding of that spiritual path needed to carefully take into account the particular struggles and realities of someone who for a while had lived in intense darkness.

*Holding on to Hope* is about learning to be receptive to God connecting with us so that God can indeed heal us—heal us, I repeat, not cure us—of depression or erase the sorrows of failure or restore lost loves. One clue to this change of posture is the chapter titles. The chapters of *Surviving Depression* are titles with quotations from people suffering with depression: "I Just Want to Feel Better"; "Why Doesn't God Heal Me?"; "I'm Going Crazy." The chapter titles for *Holding on to Hope*, on the other hand, include quotations from God, found in God's great love letter to us, the Scriptures: "Look, I'm making everything new"; "Do you want to get well?"; "Blessed are the pure in heart."

In the last three days of my retreat in Maine—when I was finally pronounced "ready" by my guide—I was put on a transformative path I could never have created on my own. This book hopes to unfold that journey for you, so that you, too, may be healed.

## Each Chapter Is a Part of the Journey

Let me explain how Sister Helene and I have set up this book. Each chapter looks at how we as humans are transformed. Each step we take in healing, spirituality, or transformation is made up of elements that complete one another: a rational element, an emotive element, a spiritual element, at times a physiological element, a divine element. We are inspired or moved on many different levels: our mind, our will, our heart—that is, on the level of our thoughts, judgments, desires, ideals, convictions, choices, decisions. In another, more popular, manner of expressing this integration of our growth, we are transformed in our mind, body, soul, and spirit. We begin to feel different, to move in a different interior space, to think differently, to perceive, intuit, and mentally frame situations differently. Our choices in everyday life, preferences, work styles, and play styles change. We find ourselves reacting to situations and persons around us in healthier ways. Emotionally we are in a better place. Our loves have deepened, changed. Our participation in spirituality and the life of God has become a more integrated part of our life. This is what Saint Paul meant by: "It is no longer I who live, but it is Christ who lives in me. And the life I now live in the flesh I live by my faith in the Son of God" (Gal 2:20 NRSV).

Thus each chapter of this book includes elements for just such a whole mind-body-soul-spirit experience that supports healing and transformative change.

## Images

Stories speak to the heart; they alone are able to steal under the traps of our mental habits and prejudices. They can inspire courage in those hearts that are most afraid or asleep. The stories, or dreams, or images presented in each chapter are narratives that directly recount an interaction with God.

## Scripture

Scripture is the divine element of the healing plan. God's word has the capacity to strike us anew in every element of our being, much as lightning strikes. Of course, it doesn't kill us, but it can gradually or immediately "kill the old man" and allow the new person within us to be free and to grow.

## Reflection Questions for Personal or Small Group Use

Questions help us explore what the text means for us, what has been prompted within us, what calls or tugs we feel in our heart, what challenges we've faced, what surprises have upset us. You'll find these in the section titled "Exploring" because these evocative questions are not meant as a test or as a review, but as a further exploration. They can be used as a type of personal journey in spiritual direction.

## Contemplative Experiences or "Listening"

Each dream or image presented in the chapter can also be a jumping-off point for interaction with God in order to truly listen to the Lord speaking deep within. These images "set the scene," so to speak, and leave the rest to the Lord who deals directly with each one of us. They can mentor a deeply prayerful relationship with God and, at the same time, a profound reevaluation and healing of our lives. For the two really go together.

## Resting

Besides the contemplation of Scripture that follows the image, three sets of Scripture passages with introductions are provided at the end of each chapter under the heading "Resting." That may seem like a curious title, but let me explain. After all the "work" of the chapter, you will need to rest. There is no better place to "rest" than in God's message to us in Scripture. These passages are placed at the end of each chapter on purpose to enable you to slow down and stop before moving on to the next. You will be able to look at the theme of the chapter from different perspectives and angles. The introductions will invite you to compare and contrast different people in the Scriptures who dealt with the issues raised by the topic in the chapter. So take three days or so and continue to contemplate the chapter before reading on. After all, a doctor can't heal you without performing the surgery required. He or she can't just talk about it, describe it, or prepare for it. The doctor needs to actually perform it, and the patient needs to undergo it. The "Resting" section could be considered the place for "divine surgery." Please resist the temptation to skip over it.

## Inner Healing Exercises

On the healing retreat mentioned in the introduction, my director, Sister Helene Cote, used many inner healing exercises that were practical tools to get me "unstuck" from my thought-choice-emotion pattern so that I could freely get on with a more whole and Christ-ed life. The section of each chapter titled "Inner Healing" is written by Sister Helene and offers truly helpful and powerful ways to integrate the topic of the chapter into your everyday life so that spirituality doesn't become or remain compartmentalized with no influence on your parenting style, business decisions, life choices, and the like.

SISTER KATHRYN HERMES

# Before You Begin

I am no stranger to the darkness of depression, and for almost twenty years I fell victim to many self-doubts, judgments, continual fatigue, and self-hatred. It was like wearing a heavy hooded coat that weighed me down and prevented me from seeing clearly, from living life to the full. After years of struggling, I began in 2000 a sabbatical time that led me on a painful and yet incredible journey of self-discovery. My life is very different now. I am truly happy and at peace. Although I am a spiritual director, and not a therapist, my hope is that the tools I share in this book (the "Inner Healing" section of each chapter), which have helped me through the years and which I have used with so many others, will help you reclaim a life filled with hope and joy.

One of the greatest truths about healing is that we cannot heal ourselves. We need God's grace (as mentioned in the Introduction) and we also need others to journey with us. One of the basic steps in healing is learning to articulate what we are feeling, what we are thinking. Therefore, you may wish to use this book with a spiritual director, a mentor, a friend, or a faith-filled therapist. If you do not have someone to share this journey with, journaling can be a meaningful way to "speak" your truth aloud.

Before starting any of the inner healing exercises found at the end of every chapter, it is always good to begin with a moment of prayer. Any form of prayer can be used, but guided imagery can be especially helpful because it allows us to use our imagination and to be open to symbols particularly valuable for us. The following can be repeated in each chapter, before the inner healing exercise.

SISTER HELENE COTE

# Guided Imagery
# Contemplative Exercise

Take some time to be quiet. Sit in a comfortable place where you will not be disturbed. If you choose, you can set the atmosphere by playing some soft instrumental music. Close your eyes. Begin by taking some deep breaths, remembering that God's Spirit surrounds you and is within you. Ask God to guide you on this inner journey. For several moments, breathe in God's Spirit and exhale any anxiety or fear or discomfort you might have. Breathe in the Spirit and let go of whatever weighs heavy on your heart.

Imagine yourself in a beautiful place in nature. It can be a real place or an imaginary one, but it is above all a place of beauty and one that is safe for you. Ground yourself in this place by using your senses. What do you see, hear, smell, feel? Savor the beauty and relax. You notice a path and you begin walking, always taking in the beauty. Eventually you see a bench and you sit down. As you sit there you allow the peace and the beauty of this place to hold you. This is your sacred space, and you can return here as often as you like. Now imagine that you are enveloped in a warm golden light. You are being held in God's loving embrace. Allow yourself to feel the warmth permeate your body. Just sit quietly and ask God for the grace to walk courageously on the path of healing and hope. Stay there as long as you like, and when your personal cloud dissipates you find yourself once again savoring the beauty around you and the encounter you have had. When you are ready, come back to the present time and place by opening your eyes. Notice what is surfacing within you. Journal and begin your inner work.

The Lord says: "Peace, peace, to the far and the near ... and I will heal them" (Isa 57:19 NRSV).

# Chapter One

# Three Basic Principles of Healing

## *"Look, I'm making everything new"*

 IMAGING

The night cloaked my room with a darkness that was penetratingly cold. The alarm clock pierced the silence with its loud, unwanted announcement of the coming sunrise. I fumbled quickly through my desk for a paper and pen to write down a dream I had had. I never remember my dreams, but this one had been too vivid to allow it to slip back into the mists of my subconscious. In my dream, I was in a room with a friend and had made it clear to her that we were not permitted under any conditions or for any reason to rearrange the furniture. While I was getting my coat in another part of the house, my friend had begun to move the furniture around with no particular attention to where the furniture landed. An immediate panic seized me when I realized my friend had not only changed the position of the bed, table, and chairs, she had created an interior decorator's nightmare.

I jotted down the seemingly simple symbols and the following week shared them with my spiritual director, who encouraged me to bring the symbol of the furniture to prayer. "The Spirit often speaks to us through dreams, especially those that are so vivid."

In our conversation we decided the panic at the moving of the furniture definitely symbolized feeling out of control as my friend challenged my stodgy life decisions. I've got everything figured out and nailed down and don't need anything new to upset things, thank you.

A tiny flicker of freedom lit up the otherwise foreboding panic of change that was symbolized by the furniture now lying helter-skelter around the room in a disorganized maze.

Through the next weeks, as I prayed, the dream image developed in my prayer and I realized that the room was flying—a symbol of transcendence—and that the door was open, that my friend in the room was actually God, that God was now pushing the furniture out the open door, and, to my horror, that God was actually trying to push me out the door. "Ah," said my spiritual director, "so God is not afraid to push the old man out the door...." I ignored the comment.

Grasping the meaning of the furniture became a contemplative odyssey. The symbol had layers of meaning. One transformative discovery I made was that the furniture symbolized my self-concept, my judgments of myself, the labels I gave myself or allowed others to give me, my self-analysis. It's the mind's job to make judgments. After everything we say or do, our mind says, "That was smart!" "Why did I say that? "What is she going to think about me now?" God was saying, "Out the door with it all. I have no use for it. It has no real meaning. It is confining both of us in a box. It is prohibiting our relationship from developing."

Since I didn't trust God enough to let him do it, I had managed to keep him from throwing me out the door. So with the furniture gone, the room was empty. Only God and I were left in the room, and I bowed before him. We were no longer separated by my mental constructs and judgments. As I remained in God's presence, I kept dropping my analyses and thoughts as they emerged, returning to a simple, receptive awareness.

## CONTEMPLATION

### *"Look, I'm making everything new" (Rev 21:5 MSG)*

The author of the Book of Revelation, believed to be John the Apostle, calls himself a prophet. At the island of Patmos he is given a series of visions that enable him to offer hope to his brothers and sisters suffering persecution in Asia Minor. The seven churches listed in the first three chapters of this book were seven cities on a single road. The book would easily have been passed from congregation to congregation and been read aloud to the Christians who needed encouragement in their suffering.

The author recounts for his fellow persecuted Christians a vision similar to those recounted in the Old Testament books of Daniel and Ezekiel. When he sees the vision of the seven lamp stands and a man holding seven stars walking among them, he falls at the man's feet. The author, who had lived through the personal, spiritual, and psychological hell of persecution and had refused to worship before the images of the emperor, now falls as if dead before this man whose hair is white as snow and whose eyes burn like flames. The man touches John with his right hand and says "Don't fear. I'm First, I'm Last, I'm Alive. I died, but I came to life, and my life is now forever" (Rev 1:17 MSG).

John, in this vision, teaches us three basic principles of healing: worship, listen, see. These three basic principles are the initial "movement of the furniture," so to speak, that begin our healing.

## Worship

First, God breaks through our self-concepts, in sometimes unsettling ways, in order to reveal himself to us. God acts firmly, taking things into his own hands (and out of ours). We may cry in these first stages. One day, however, he will wipe away our tears. God is not afraid "to push the old man out the door," to mess up the organization of our lives—what we think we are capable of doing, our plans that keep our fears at bay, the control we have asserted over others for our own self-protection.

The response God waits for is worship, because ultimately it is not we who make new lives for ourselves. It is God, who just as he will create new heavens and a new earth, makes us new.

So long as our response to having our life shaken up remains anger—a perfectly understandable human reaction—healing can't commence. Therapy can help us with the anger. A spiritual director can explore with us our image of God. But eventually we ourselves need to decide to worship.

## Listen

Second, when we take the risk to worship, we listen to Jesus' voice saying, "Don't be afraid. I'm here. I control everything. I am the Beginning and the End. I died and am now alive for ever and ever." For the persecuted Christians, threatened with execution for refusing to worship the Roman emperor, to hear the voice of One who died saying that now he controls the passageways of death, was to hear hope. Now he lives. Death is not forever. Death has been overcome. Their death also has been overcome. They are held gently in their sufferings and borne into eternal life.

Depression, betrayal, illness, failure are deaths in so many ways. Many lose their name, their marriage, their families, their friends, their careers, their self-esteem, their confidence in life. To them and to us Jesus says, "Fear is useless. I'm here. I died, too. I am now alive forever and ever."

## See

Third, Jesus invites us to look up and see the One who is saying to us, "I Am." We need to stop looking at ourselves—the labels we put on ourselves, our self-analysis, our judgments—and begin looking instead at the One who says: I am the First. I am the Last. I am Alpha. I am Omega. I am Forever. There is something larger than your illness. I have a greater part to play in your life than what you are suffering. I know all about you. I have designs for your life, and illness or disaster will not stop me from making of you something beautiful and meaningful.

Truly the only labels I am allowed to have about myself or others, even about the Church, are those of God. I see myself accurately only when I see myself or others through God's eyes.

It is important to move beyond a vague concept of God to a more concrete understanding of God-With-Us in the person of Jesus Christ. Just as the Church was in the first century, we too are grasped by the powerful hand of the Risen Christ who walks in our midst as the conqueror of death.

—⟡— EXPLORING —⟡—

•✦• Not all dreams are messages of God; some are just dreams, or nightmares. However, some dreams can be signposts for important shifts in our life. Have you ever had a significant dream? Can you recall any details? Have you prayed with this image, or could you do so now? Have dreams ever been moments of self-discovery? In what way?

- Has a broken relationship, misunderstanding, personal betrayal, disaster, or emotional disorder affected your self-image? In what way? Can you identify self-concepts that may be preventing joy or hindering growth? In what ways, if any, have these been a death for you? What would happen if you "pushed them out the door"?

- Could you practice contemplative wonder? What would happen if you became aware of your judgments and analyses, gently discarding them as they arise? Try to stay present to the now, receiving each breath, each moment, enjoying it while you have it, and letting it go. What difference does this practice make in your attitude?

- Was there a time when God was working in your life and it made you cry? What was that like? Were your tears wiped away? Transformed? What were the circumstances of this goodness on God's part?

- On a scale of one to ten, how much do you control your life, other's lives? How do you exercise this control of yourself, situations, others? What benefits do you receive from keeping things under control? What would happen if you let go? What would be the worst thing that would happen if you did? What are possible positive consequences of letting go?

- In what area of your life might God be asking you to relinquish control? How does this make you feel? What is your first reaction? Why? What would it take for you to be able to worship God who is making something new of your life?

## — LISTENING —

When you have an extended time to go deep within your heart, either imagine yourself with John on Patmos or in some other quiet place where you can meet God—a favorite secluded spot in nature, a vacation spot, a sacred place in a church or monastery. Imagine that Jesus comes to you. Angels surround you with song, and they bow at his feet, covering their faces. Take the risk to bow also. Feel what it is to bow before him, to remain at his feet in adoration and trust. Tell Jesus what you are feeling. "Jesus, this is so...." Or, "Jesus, I feel like...." When you are finished, stand up, look into his eyes, and wait for him to speak to you.

## — RESTING —

Resting with the following passages of Scripture can deepen your healing. To prepare your heart to rest where this deep healing can truly take place, repeat the above listening prayer experience before using any of these Scripture passages. Then choose a passage and place yourself into the scene it describes. Each time tell Jesus what you see and what you feel, and wait for him to say something to you.

### Dreams

Genesis 28:10–22
Matthew 1:18–25

Two famous dreamers in Scripture are Jacob (in the Old Testament) and Joseph (in the New Testament). Both Jacob and Joseph found themselves in a mess that could have led to deep depression. Jacob had deceived his father and stolen his brother's birthright. Now alone, he is fleeing his brother, leaving family and homeland, and God gives him a dream assuring him of his future (cf. Gen 28:10–22). Joseph was espoused to Mary, and suddenly found out that she was going to have a baby. The Law said she should be stoned. He loved her and didn't want to see her put to death. He was trapped between his love for God and his love for his wife-to-be. God intervened one night in a dream and explained to him the new direction his life was to take (cf. Mt 1:18–25).

Jacob's dream:

> Know that I am with you and will keep you wherever you go, and will bring you back to this land; for I will not leave you until I have done what I have promised you. (Gen 28:15 NRSV)

Joseph's dream:

> An angel of the Lord appeared to him in a dream and said, "Joseph, son of David, do not be afraid to take Mary as your wife, for the child conceived in her is from the Holy Spirit. She will bear a son, and you are to name him Jesus, for he will save his people from their sins." (Mt 1:20–21 NRSV)

## Control

Genesis 12:1–9
Exodus 3:7–10

Both Abraham and Moses had their lives interrupted. Abraham amassed a fortune and had settled down comfortably for the rest of his life (cf. Gen 12:1–9). Moses tried to take control over the destiny of his people by murdering one of their oppressors, then fled to the desert to escape capital punishment (cf. Ex 2:11–3:10).

To both of these men God said, "I am going to do something new in the world, and guess who is going to help me!"

Abraham:

> Now the LORD said to Abram, "Go from your country and your kindred and your father's house to the land that I will show you. I will make of you a great nation, and I will bless you, and make your name great, so that you will be a blessing. I will bless those who bless you, and the one who curses you I will curse; and in you all the families of the earth shall be blessed." (Gen 12:1–3 NRSV)

Moses:

> "So come, I will send you to Pharaoh to bring my people, the Israelites, out of Egypt." (Ex 3:10 NRSV)

## Worship, Listen, See

John 8:2–11
John 20:11–18

Those who came in contact with Jesus often had their lives disrupted. The so-named "woman caught in adultery" is brought before Jesus with a humiliating accusation. The labels applied to her melt away in the presence of Love Incarnate. She has to begin to know herself in new ways. She has to look into the eyes of Jesus who challenges her to become who she is in his eyes (cf. Jn 8:2–11). Mary Magdalene, in the garden after the resurrection, finding the tomb empty, is another woman who faces the most terrifying experience of letting go of control. Not only does she have to let go of any hope of protecting someone she loves from danger, she sees the hope of the Messiah's promises disintegrate around her. The group of disciples who had been close as they followed the Master is now gone. She has no control over the future of her own life. It seems that everything is gone (cf. Jn 20:11–18).

The woman caught in adultery:

> Jesus straightened up and said to her, "Woman, where are they? Has no one condemned you?" She said, "No one, sir." And Jesus said, "Neither do I condemn you. Go your way, and from now on do not sin again." (Jn 8:10–11 NRSV)

Mary in the garden of the resurrection:

> But Mary stood weeping outside the tomb. As she wept, she bent over to look into the tomb; and she saw two angels in white, sitting where the body of Jesus had been lying.... They said to her, "Woman, why are you weeping?" She said to them, "They have taken away my Lord, and I do not know where they have laid him." (Jn 20:11–13 NRSV)

## INNER HEALING

Before beginning this section you may wish to pray with the guided imagery contemplation found on page 9.

Almost everyone at some point in life struggles with insurmountable problems that could lead to discouragement, frustration, and even depression. In whatever way these situations appear, self-doubts, judgments, and self-hatred often become part and parcel of life. Most of the judgments we make about ourselves and others are rooted in words and experiences from our childhood. Our parents, grandparents, teachers, and other significant adults play a great role in shaping the thoughts we have about ourselves and the way we think the world "should be." Some of our beliefs come from statements we heard such as "You're always in the way," or "You'll never amount to anything." Sometimes the thoughts come from the way we interpreted events from a child's perspective. For example, if adults were so busy working that they never had time for us, despite the fact that they loved us, we may have inferred that "I am not important." If no one ever stopped to listen to what we had to say, we may believe "My opinion or my voice doesn't count." If we were raised in a dysfunctional environment, the message we got was probably "Don't talk, don't trust, don't feel."

I call these thoughts "the committee." Some of these thoughts are helpful and lead us to be cautious, to learn from past mistakes, to run from danger, and to protect ourselves. Some, however, are negative thoughts we have believed our whole life, and they need to be reevaluated and reframed in order to be more in line with the truth. It is helpful to share with someone while we are reframing our thoughts, someone trustworthy and who can help us look at statements that come from "the committee."

When you are upset or discouraged, what are some negative statements you tell yourself? Make a list of these. Next, write beside each thought, when you first began to think this way about yourself, whom these thoughts come from or what situation led you to think this about yourself. How could you reframe that statement to be more in line with the truth? Write the reframed statement. For example, the thought "Everything I do is wrong" can be reframed as "Sometimes I make mistakes, but often what I do comes out well." Work with one or two statements at a time, perhaps starting with those you repeat most often. When you catch yourself thinking one of these negative statements, STOP! Replace it immediately with a new, more positive statement.

Everything begins with the thoughts we believe about ourselves. These thoughts shape our feelings, and the feelings impact the way we will act or react to situations. To change or heal our lives, we must begin by revisiting some of our beliefs about ourselves and about the way things "should" be.

Chapter Two

# Seeing in New Ways

*"Do you want to get well?"*

 IMAGING

The day had been a long one. I was overly anxious. Darkness and negativity clung to everything I touched. Irritability encroached around the edges of my conversations. I was tired and knew that that night I wouldn't be able to sleep. Since I have epilepsy, like many other men and women in the world today, I can count on having these lifelong companions: depression, anxiety, irritability, insomnia. Psychological vulnerabilities such as these shape our thought patterns and expectations, and in turn these negative thoughts create the dark world we sometimes believe exists around us. Our world is created mostly by what is inside our heads. What we see is determined by what we believe.

When circumstances in our life are dim, it is easy to let our thinking degenerate into fragmentation. The result is criticism; moralizing; attacks on other people or ideas, opinions, or events; negativity; anxiety; and agitation, the belief that fear, and not love, is the compelling force of the universe. It takes mental "muscle" to be responsible for our thinking, to think thoughts of wholeness, care, and healing. For example, it is easy for me to see problems, to hear voices that are complaining about things that I do, to notice who is not happy with me. Because this is the way I think about myself, this is what I notice in the world around me. When I begin to change the way I think, to indulge in thoughts of appreciation and beauty, goodness, and peace, I suddenly begin to notice that others appreciate me and that the strident complainers are really very few. I discover that I didn't have all the information—and usually I am missing the most important information—to assess a person or situation accurately. When I find out the truth I feel bad that I have judged myself or another harshly with unforgiveness in my heart.

Fragmented, belittling, or negative thinking dehumanizes us and lowers the worth of others in our eyes. It creates division, whereas, in reality, as sons and daughters of God, we are already one.

All of us have been in meetings where the group has trashed someone's project or reputation, a leader's track record or decision, or the group's purpose or history. When I am a part of such a situation, even simply as an unwilling listener who is sharing air space with negative hearts, I begin to close down. The razor-sharp accusations seem to make so much sense as they are presented, but I begin to feel as though I can't breathe. Any hopeful future is choked off as the group becomes more and more demoralized. The Spirit is not a part of that conversation. These destructive, distorted statements both reveal people's inner world and create their outer environment. They close off new possibilities.

We can always choose to see the world differently. In dark times it is imperative that we pay attention to how we look at the world, others, and ourselves. As we choose peace of mind, our perceptions will change. When judgment ceases, healing occurs. When we tear up the scripts we have written for how we believe we or others should be, speak, or act, we become loving and open. We can choose to see our present upset in another way. Healthy change begins to happen as we soften and mellow under the warmth of God's grace. It will mean giving up the all-American sense of entitlement to what I "deserve" or "have a right to" in order to live in a detached appreciation for the truth, goodness, and beauty I discover around me. Healing can happen only if there is a certain simplicity about how I go about living and relating and working.

## CONTEMPLATION

*"Do you want to get well?" (Jn 5:6 NRSV)*

In the Gospels Jesus often asks seemingly useless questions. He asks a blind man, "Do you want to see?" He asks a leper, "What do you want me to do for you?" He asks a man who had been sick for thirty-eight years and is sitting by the side of the sheep pool, "Do you want to be made well?" What answer was Jesus expecting?

The fifth chapter of John's Gospel recounts Jesus curing a man who had been sick for a long time. He walks into a group of people by a pool in Bethesda who are waiting for a healing, zeroes in on one individual, and asks him, "Do you want to be healed?" We might imagine that the man would immediately say, YES! But instead he lists the reasons why he can't be healed. His frame of reference is confined to the healing waters at Bethesda where he has come with the hope of finding a cure.

Instead of a cure, the man has found only a bunch of people looking out for themselves who haven't been able to help him get into the restoring water. Jesus doesn't pay attention to any of those details. He simply states: "Get up now. You can walk home from here a new man."

From the words of the man who caught Jesus' eye at Bethesda, it seems that everyone there was out for himself. The Gospel says the man had been there for thirty-eight years (that's just twelve years shy of half a century)! Others had presumably gotten to the water ahead of him, been healed, and left for a new life. There is no mention of someone staying behind to help out anyone else. Indeed, the sick man states, "Sir, I have no one to put me into the pool when the water is stirred up; and while I am making my way, someone else steps down ahead of me." His thought patterns and expectations are closing him off to the possibilities of a different type of healing offered by the man (by God) who stands right in front of him and asks him: May I cure you? Will you let me? He can't imagine that Jesus could operate outside the possibilities known to him.

Jesus simply tells him, "Pick up your mat and walk" (Jn 5:8 NIV). Jesus shows us that something beyond our wildest imagining can break open our world and change us completely.

Those of us who suffer with depression, if we have minds filled frequently with chaos or weary with the struggle to keep us on an even keel, could, like the man by the sheep pool, also have a worldview that has become too small. The attempt to just survive can contract our personal universe to a "safe" size. Our thinking patterns can become caught in overcontrolled ruts. We lose flexibility in favor of the fight/flight/freeze mechanism that leads to hypervigilance and shutdown.

If Jesus were to come upon us today and ask, "Do you want to be healed?" we might also recount our life stories and point out to him what hasn't worked. A couple years ago, when I first started meeting with Father Dave, my spiritual director, he would ask me a question and I would begin to recount for him a psychological analysis of why I do this, or feel that, or can't get beyond something else. After a while he said, "I have a feeling Jesus wants to heal you, and he's not going to need to know your therapeutic analysis. So let's stop all that and start looking at what Jesus is doing." It took me awhile to switch gears from self-analysis to contemplative observation. I needed to learn to see Jesus standing right in front of me saying, lovingly and gently, "Get up. Be healed."

Holding on to hope requires that we flood our mind and spirit with a transcendent light, that we see things as they truly are, bathed in God's gentle love and care. It means thinking differently: looking for unity not fragmentation, appreciation not complaints, simplicity not entitlement, hope not despair. What we think creates the world around us.

## EXPLORING

- Is depression or some other psychological vulnerability a part of your everyday life? Are you living through painful circumstances that you hadn't anticipated? What effect does this have on your thought patterns? On the way you see others or events?

- Have you experienced that your world is created mostly by what is inside your head? What did you learn from this experience?

- Do you find yourself often disappointed by others who haven't lived up to your expectations, what you want them to be? Who or what do you want to be different than it is? What would happen if you stopped writing scripts about these things and accepted them as they are? How would that alter the way you look at your own life?

- What changes might happen in your life if you focused on developing thoughts of love and forgiveness? Do your manner and behavior put a smile on the face of everyone you meet?

- Are you depressing to be around because of complaining or blaming? How could you reach out to help others? To whom could you give your heart? When you give of yourself to others or to a cause, complaining and blaming disappear.

- Are your thought patterns and expectations closing you off from the possibility of something different? Is there someone or something in your life right now offering you a new direction? What's preventing you from taking it?

- Can you practice thinking thoughts of love, healing, and peace? What difference does that make in your attitude? In your life?

- How would you know if Jesus was addressing you today, desiring to offer you new possibilities for spiritual growth and personal healing?

## LISTENING

Stand beside the sick man at the pool of Bethesda. In your imagination, picture yourself as a sick person in the midst of the crowd of people longing for a cure. Take a moment to look around. Who else is there? What do you hear? What is your story? Why are you there? What cure are you hoping for? Listen to the conversation between the sick man and Jesus. As the sick man stands, picks up his mat, and leaves, reach up to get Jesus' attention. As he looks at you, he asks you, "What is it that you desire?" Speak to Jesus and wait for him to respond.

## RESTING

Resting with these passages of Scripture can deepen your healing. To prepare yourself to rest deeply in your heart where healing can truly take place, you can repeat the listening prayer experience above before you use any of these Scripture passages, or you can place yourself into the scene described in the passage. Each time, tell Jesus what you see and what you feel, and wait for him to say something to you.

### New Life Possibilities

Jeremiah 1:4–10
Luke 1:5–25

Jesus often asks people, "What do you desire?" or "Do you want to be healed?" But just as often he comes to a person who has his own plan for his life, her own dreams for her future. In both Jeremiah's call (cf. Jer 1:4–10) and the announcement that Zechariah's wife would give birth to a special child who was to be named John (cf. Lk 1:5–25), the desire and the dream are God's. The vocation he gives to both of these men—the call to be prophet and father—is intimately tied to mission. It is for the sake of others. In the face of God's dream we have different reactions: I am afraid. I am too young. How is this going to happen? This doesn't make sense. Are you sure? You duped me. When human meets divine we struggle within the mystery of something so much larger than we could ever conceive on our own. It is because we are meant to exist for others, to live in the drama of life among and with others. Jeremiah's excuse:

"Before I formed you in the womb I knew you,
and before you were born I consecrated you,
I appointed you a prophet to the nations."
Then I said, "Ah, LORD God! Truly I do not know how to
speak, for I am only a boy."

But the LORD said to me,
"Do not say, 'I am only a boy';
for you shall go to all to whom I send you,
and you shall speak whatever I command you.
Do not be afraid of them,
for I am with you to deliver you, says the LORD."
(Jer 1:5–8 NRSV)

Zechariah's vision:

> Then there appeared to him an angel of the Lord, standing at
> the right side of the altar of incense. When Zechariah saw
> him, he was terrified; and fear overwhelmed him. But the
> angel said to him, "Do not be afraid, Zechariah, for your
> prayer has been heard. Your wife Elizabeth will bear you a son,
> and you will name him John. You will have joy and gladness,
> and many will rejoice at his birth. . . . He will turn many of the
> people of Israel to the LORD their God." (Lk 1:11–16 NRSV)

## Our Thoughts Limit Our World

John 3:1–21
Matthew 6:7–13

Some of the religious leaders in John's Gospel approach the
"problem" of Jesus' popularity with a simple solution: Jesus has
to prove to their satisfaction that he is who he says he is. They
become the judges of the Redeemer, the judges of the Judge of
the world. Their traditions, their understanding, their personal
ideas become the measure with which they measure God. And
God doesn't fit. The account of Nicodemus' conversation with

Jesus is enlightening. He tells Jesus, "Well, I have decided you must be a teacher come from God." Jesus doesn't say, "Thank you for your vote of confidence." He tells the well-meaning Pharisee, "Your scholarly assessment really tells you little about me. You need to become a child. In fact, you need to be born again." Now that doesn't match Nicodemus' vocabulary or fit into his plans at all. In fact, he doesn't understand what Jesus means. And he couldn't until he has let all he has learned and thought and concluded fall away so he could be instructed anew. He needs to become a child (cf. Jn 3:1–21). In fact, Jesus is not asking something he himself has not done. He too has become "a child," born of a woman as we are, and has remained the child of his Father with trust, obedience, and love his whole life. It is into this childhood that Jesus invites us with the prayer he taught us (cf. Mt 6:7–13).

Nicodemus:

> Jesus answered him, "Very truly, I tell you, no one can see the kingdom of God without being born from above." Nicodemus said to him, "How can anyone be born after having grown old? Can one enter a second time into the mother's womb and be born?" Jesus answered, "Very truly, I tell you, no one can enter the kingdom of God without being born of water and Spirit. What is born of the flesh is flesh, and what is born of the Spirit is spirit. Do not be astonished that I said to you, 'You must be born from above. . . .'" Nicodemus said to him, "How can these things be?" Jesus answered him, "Are you a teacher of Israel, and yet you do not understand these things?" (Jn 3:3–10 NRSV)

Jesus:

> Your Father knows what you need before you ask him.
> Pray then in this way:
> Our Father in heaven,

hallowed be your name.
Your kingdom come.... (Mt 6:8–10 NRSV)

## Healing Thoughts

1 Corinthians 13:1–13
Colossians 3:12–17

I can tell you the moment when my airtight, anxious, self-serving mental world was punctured. I can recount the conversation and list who I was with. It was a moment of freedom. I could finally move beyond my idea of certainty, my view of reality, to see things from another's perspective. At that moment it became crystal clear what Paul meant when he said that no matter how smart, how talented, how philanthropic he was, if he didn't love, he was nothing. Love changes us—not just a basic kindly attitude, but the virtue that, first, puts us in our humble place in relation to one another (cf. 1 Cor 13:1–13) and, second, leads us to sacrifice ourselves for another because we ourselves have been loved in this way (cf. Col 3:12–17).

> If I speak in the tongues of mortals and of angels, but do not have love, I am a noisy gong or a clanging cymbal. And if I have prophetic powers, and understand all mysteries and all knowledge, and if I have all faith, so as to remove mountains, but do not have love, I am nothing. If I give away all my possessions, and if I hand over my body so that I may boast, but do not have love, I gain nothing.... And now faith, hope, and love abide, these three; and the greatest of these is love. (1 Cor 13:1–3; 13 NRSV)

> As God's chosen ones, holy and beloved, clothe yourselves with compassion, kindness, humility, meekness, and patience. Bear with one another and, if anyone has a complaint against another, forgive each other; just as the Lord has forgiven you. (Col 3:12–13 NRSV)

## ⸻ INNER HEALING ⸻

Before beginning this section you may wish to pray with the guided imagery contemplation found on page 9.

In his book *The Hidden Messages of Water*, Masaru Emoto, a Japanese scientist and original thinker, shows that water crystals are affected by pollution and the vibrational energy of music and even words. By photographing water crystals that have been exposed to pollution, various types of music, and words of love and peace or, alternatively, anger and hate, he was able to observe that water absorbs energy and the energy is reflected in the crystals when frozen. The most beautiful and unique crystals are formed when exposed to the energy of loving and peaceful words. Words of anger and hatred produce deformed and broken crystals.[1]

Whatever the scientific explanation of Emoto's research, we have always known this intuitively: when we are in an atmosphere that is tense and filled with angry words and attitudes, we are affected not only emotionally, but physically as well. This in part explains how the voices of "the committee" can drag us down even physically. When we are nurtured with a loving atmosphere, with positive affirmations, our whole being benefits. We absorb the positive energy, and we feel more alive and at peace with who we are.

Prayer is one place where we can immerse ourselves in love and peace, for the benefit of our whole being. Choose one short phrase from Scripture, or an affirmation that has meaning for you, and imagine that God is speaking these words to you or that you are speaking them to God. Receive this power and repeat it as often as you can during the day. You may want to use your

---

1. See www.hado.net.

rosary and on each bead repeat these wonderful statements. What is most important is that we feed our minds and hearts with the memory of how we are loved unconditionally by God. Here are a few phrases from Scripture (by no means an exhaustive list). You might find it helpful to write your favorite phrases in a journal.

"You are precious in my eyes and glorious, and I love you" (Isa 43:4 NAB). This could be adapted to: I am precious in God's eyes, and God loves me.

"Fear is useless. What is needed is trust" (Mk 5:36 NAB).

"Take courage! I have overcome the world" (Jn 16:33 NAB). Adapted: Take courage! Jesus has overcome the world!

"You are my beloved Son. On you my favor rests" (Lk 3:22 NAB). Adapted: I am God's beloved child. On me God's favor rests.

"There is nothing I cannot do with the help of the One who gives me strength" (Phil 4:13 NJB).

Chapter Three

# Throwing Yourself
# upon the Resources of God

## *"Eat this scroll"*

Words ... images ... gestures ... We communicate with each other using all three. God also communicates with us in this way, inspiring our minds, moving our wills, inflaming our hearts. Often, however, the most powerful way God communicates is through images. Perhaps God and we use images because often images convey more than concepts. They burrow down beneath thoughts, rationalizations, explanations, and logic, finding their way into the heart of the listener. They reveal emotion and evoke response.

An image I once prayed with was the image of a meadow. My "flying house," from chapter one, did eventually land, and I found myself in a meadow, an image I sought to explore with God. After doing a quick search, I found two places in the *New International Version* translation where the word "meadow" appears. The first appearance is in the Book of Isaiah, chapter 44.

Verse 4 reads: "They will spring up like grass in a meadow, like poplar trees by flowing streams."

In the previous chapter, Isaiah the prophet recounts God's promises and also his pain. God promises the miracle of a new exodus to the Israelite people who are exiled in Babylon. It was almost as if God was saying, "You remember being told of the exodus from Egypt when I led your fathers to safety through the Red Sea? That is nothing compared with the way I will deliver you from your exile and bring you back to Zion."

The text then switches abruptly to God expressing his pain over Israel's ingratitude. "You have not invoked me, you have not offered sacrifices, you have grown weary of me."

God's next words are the most beautiful: "And, now, listen." Notice that the word used here is "and," not "but." You have treated me badly, and I am now going to do something marvelous for you. This "and" expresses a love more marvelous than the love of a parent or a spouse could ever be: a love that does not shame. God doesn't say: "You have been ungrateful, but I'm still going to be faithful. See how good I am?" No. It is as if God says: "You have been negligent in your religious duties toward me. And now listen because I am going to do something for you more wonderful than you could ever imagine. I am going to pour out water on the thirsty soil of your souls and create streams that will flow through the dry ground of your lives. I am going to pour my spirit into you. And then you will spring up like grass in a meadow. I will make it impossible for you not to worship and love and know and obey, because my Spirit will be in you."

When we are desperate, it is easy to dance back and forth across the line that divides asking from demanding, love from control. However, God says to the Israelites through Isaiah that he will give us a gift that we didn't even think to ask for. God will make us spring up like grass in the meadow: fresh, clean, alive, new, reaching to the sun, carefree, waving in the wind. God does for us what we can't do for ourselves because God loves us so much. "And, now, listen to what I will do for you."

## CONTEMPLATION

### *"Eat this scroll" (Ezek 3:3 NRSV)*

Ezekiel was a prophet of the exile. He was most likely among the leading people of Jerusalem deported with the royal family in 597 B.C. when the Babylonians partially ransacked the Temple. The disoriented and humiliated exiles began a new life. Some of the exiles were settled in Tel-abib (cf. Ezek 3:15). For these elite exiles, used to luxury and wealth, this must have been a bitter and disorienting experience. After a fresh uprising of the Judeans who had remained in Jerusalem in 586, the Temple of Jerusalem was burned and torn to the ground. The majority of the people left in the city were deported.

Ezekiel had received his prophetic call in 593, in the midst of what seemed to be the final destruction of the Chosen People, their irreversible rejection by the Lord. With the destruction of the Temple, the place where the Lord had made himself present in the midst of his people, they were tempted to believe that they had no more claim on the heart of God who had called their father Abraham from the land of the Chaldeans, led them forth from Egypt under the leadership of Moses, solidified their possession of the Chosen Land through the military prowess of King David, and come to reside in his glory in the Temple built by Solomon. Now the Temple was no more, and the Israelites were finally able to understand the words of the prophets who had warned them for hundreds of years to return to the Lord and stop their idolatrous ways and unjust practices. But they had awakened too late. Now, they feared, would the Lord ever relent? Would he forgive? For the sake of Abraham, Jacob, Moses, David, and Solomon would he reestablish them as his people in the land he had promised their fathers? Or was their glorious heritage to be lost as they were absorbed into Babylonian culture? They were tempted to give up hope. But Ezekiel assumed the prophet's role of speaking truth and hope to them.

When the Lord called Ezekiel he gave him a scroll covered with the words of the Lord and told him to take it and eat it. Ezekiel ate the scroll; a symbol of the prophet's nourishing himself on the Lord's words. These words became a part of him, and Ezekiel was transformed. These words gave him the possibility of seeing what God was going to do for his people. For a people as good as dead, the Lord was going to open their graves and breathe into them his Spirit that they might live.

When we nourish ourselves on the word of God we gradually are able to see an unexpected, unearned future: new life, a new heart, a new future, a new relationship with God. The word of the Lord became a part of Ezekiel's being, and it can become a part of our being as well. When we regularly digest God's word, options become available to us that we couldn't anticipate.

Where do we find God's words? The most obvious place is in Scripture. In days filled with stormy clouds and winds blowing chaos around us, we may come to believe things about ourselves that are untrue. We may have recurrences of low moods, irritation, and discouragement. We may find ourselves feeling very "up" or "down" for no apparent reason. We may feel more emotionally fragile than others, and come to the conclusion that we aren't normal. If emotional illness or depression is a part of our life, we may struggle with it for many long years. We may label ourselves until we, like Saint Francis who spoke of death as Sister Death, are able to address our depression as "Brother Depression," a cherished companion on our life's journey.

Even when the clouds pass we may still have a poor view of everything. We may see only the negative and believe mostly bad things without realizing how much this affects our outlook on life, relationships with others, or our disposition toward God. Our thoughts could be based not on reality but on misconception. Ezekiel teaches us that we need to "eat the scroll," nourish ourselves on the word of God in order to train our thoughts rightly, hear the truth, and hope for the future. Each of the disordered thought patterns we have learned needs to be confronted with God's truth.

Disordered thought: *God has abandoned me.*

Truth that God speaks to me:

> Do not be afraid, for I am with you;
> do not be alarmed, for I am your God.
> I give you strength, truly I help you,
> truly I hold you firm
> with my saving right hand. (Isa 41:10 JB)

Disordered thought: *There is no hope for me.*

Truth that God speaks to me:

> When you pass through the waters,
> I will be with you;
> and when you pass through the rivers,
> they will not sweep over you.
> When you walk through the fire,
> you will not be burned;
> the flames will not set you ablaze.
> For I am the LORD, your God,
> the Holy One of Israel, your Savior. (Isa 43:2–3 NIV)

Disordered thought: *I'm not needed, unimportant, unwanted.*
Truth that God speaks to me:

> It's in Christ that we find out who we are and what we are liv-
> ing for. Long before we first heard of Christ and got our hopes
> up, he had his eye on us, had designs on us for glorious living,
> part of the overall purpose he is working out in everything and
> everyone. (Eph 1:11–12 MSG)

Disordered thought: *I hate myself.*
Truth that God speaks to me:

> Are you tired? Worn out? Come to me. Get away with me and
> you'll recover your life. I'll show you how to take a real rest.
> Walk with me and work with me—watch how I do it. Learn
> the unforced rhythms of grace. I won't lay anything heavy or
> ill-fitting on you. Keep company with me and you'll learn to
> live freely and lightly. (Mt 11:28–30 MSG)

The interesting thing about Ezekiel, as with several other
prophets, is that he didn't just announce God's message with
words. He knew that words can be heard and sometimes even
understood, but they aren't always powerful enough to change
lives, to move hearts, to open up futures. Ezekiel is known for his
use of images or signs. One famous image found in the book of
Ezekiel is that of the dry bones. He is taken in spirit to a plain
filled with dry bones—skeletons that must have reminded him of
the terror of those days when Jerusalem had been sacked and he,
along with the leaders of the people, had been led through the
gates of the city, surrounded by the corpses on all sides, never to
return. To these bones the Lord tells Ezekiel to prophesy that
God will bring the dead bones to life, that he will breathe into
them his Spirit and give them life again. Ezekiel doesn't preach
self-improvement plans or strategies for growth. He tells them
what God is going to do for them, plain and simple. Though the

Israelites feel there is no hope, God is promising to act on their behalf. Thrown upon the resources of God they are to experience a spiritual transformation that will bring them back to an ever closer relationship with him.

We, too, may need images to make sense of the words, images to appropriate the message of God. A friend who is a campus minister once shared with me the story of a retreat he had offered for college seniors combined with a weekend camping trip. One evening after dark, the seniors gathered around a campfire, and my friend spoke about the Blessed Mother and how she had a special relationship with each one of them. Then he asked them to close their eyes, imagine the Blessed Mother near them, and give her a gift. After a while, each of the seniors shared the gift they had given her. Some gave her a flower. Others gave her a precious jewel. One senior said he had found it difficult to think of a gift. "What do you give to a woman who has everything?" he said. So after some thought, he gave her his grandmother's rosary beads that he had been given as a child. Then the seniors were instructed to close their eyes again and to let Mary give them a gift. As the fire was dying down and the embers glowing, each shared what gift Mary had given them. The young man who had given Mary his grandmother's rosary beads had also received a gift from Mary. She had placed it into his hand and closed it before he could see what it was. When he opened his hand, he found a piece of charcoal. Looking at Mary he asked, "You gave me a piece of charcoal?" He told his classmates with him on retreat that Mary said to him, "Yes, my son." She took the piece of charcoal from his hand, threw it into the sky, and it broke apart and became a shower of diamonds. "Yes. Because you are my diamond!" An image, a sign, can also be a means through which God moves us, transforms us, heals us, consoles us.

## EXPLORING

- Do you have any images that you frequently pray with? What are they? How have they affected the direction of your thinking? The way you look at yourself or others?

- Do you agree that sometimes we can treat God as a slave? What is the difference between asking and demanding?

- When days are difficult, how do you pray? In what ways is it difficult or easy? Do you feel a disconnect between God and you? Can you explore this disconnect now?

- Have you experienced the power of the word of God in your life? Is there a Scripture passage that has meant a lot to you in your journey? Have you made that passage a building block of your relationship with God? Do you have practical ways of reminding yourself often of it?

- Do you have negative ways of thinking that are undermining your happiness? Is there a pattern to them? Have you found a passage from Scripture, a song, a chapter of a book, or a word from a friend that can help speak truth to those disordered thoughts?

- Is it easy for you to pray with your imagination? What images have been meaningful to you in your life as you have journeyed through difficult times?

- How has God moved you? Consoled you? Transformed you?

## LISTENING

Find a quiet and sacred spot to pray. Tell Jesus that you hope to meet him there. Ask him to be present to you in a special way. Reflecting on where you are in your life, your past experiences, your hopes and dreams, your struggles and fears, decide on a gift to give Jesus. The gift should be something meaningful to you and should arise out of the context of your life experience. In your imagination, picture yourself giving this gift to Jesus. What happens when you give this gift to Jesus? Does he respond? Does he say something to you? Then wait.... Wait for Jesus to give you a gift in return.

## RESTING

Resting with these passages of Scripture can deepen your healing. To prepare yourself to rest deeply in your heart where healing can truly take place, you can repeat the listening prayer experience above before you use any of these Scripture passages, or you can place yourself into the scene described in the passage. Each time tell Jesus what you see and what you feel, and wait for him to say something to you.

### See, I Am Doing Something New!

Isaiah 43:15–21
Luke 17:12–14

At the beginning of one retreat, my director kept repeating this phrase from Isaiah, even giving it to me for meditation the first day. God says, "I am going to do something new: something new with your life; something new with your health; something new with your family; something new with your dreams." At the time it was hard to believe that something new could happen. I was stuck in a pattern of work that had become second nature. I wanted out, but my body seemed to drag my spirit into autopilot. To make a long story short, God did indeed do something unexpected, something refreshingly, surprisingly new! (cf. Isa 43:15–21). In the Gospel of Luke, ten lepers had the courage to hope for something new and cried out, "Jesus, Master, have mercy on us." Watch. God wants to do something new in your life (cf. Lk 17:12–14).

God:

> I am the LORD, your Holy One,
> the Creator of Israel, your King.…
> Do not remember the former things,
> or consider the things of old.
> I am about to do a new thing;
> now it springs forth, do you not perceive it?
> (Isa 43:15, 18–19 NRSV)

The ten lepers:

> As he entered a village, ten lepers approached him. Keeping their distance, they called out, saying, "Jesus, Master, have mercy on us!" When he saw them, he said to them, "Go and show yourselves to the priests." And as they went, they were made clean. (Lk 17:12–14 NRSV)

## God Reached Down from On High and Took Hold of Me

Psalm 18:1–19
Luke 8:22–25

A friend of mine shared Psalm 18 with me after I had first begun therapy. She wrote verses of the psalm on the back of a holy card and gave it to me as an act of faith. It has remained, since then, one of my favorite pieces of Scripture. It is full of drama: the Lord from his temple hears the cry of the psalmist; the earth trembles; he mounts the cherubim and soars on the wings of the wind; the Lord's voice thunders from heaven; he reaches down from heaven and grasps hold of the psalmist, rescuing him from the deep waters. Drama runs through the pages of Scripture if we have eyes to see it. The account of Jesus sleeping in the boat while his apostles are frantically figuring out what to do is another dramatic passage (cf. Lk 8:22–25). The events of our own lives—the failures, the risks, the depressions, the surprises—are just as dramatic and are equally places where the divine Presence can reach down from on high to take hold of us.

The psalmist's plea:

> In my distress I called upon the LORD;
> to my God I cried for help.
> From his temple he heard my voice,
> and my cry to him reached his ears. (Ps 18:6 NRSV)

Jesus in the boat:

> A gale swept down on the lake, and the boat was filling with water, and they were in danger. They went to him and woke him up, shouting, "Master, Master, we are perishing!" And he woke up and rebuked the wind and the raging waves; they ceased, and there was a calm. (Lk 8:23–24 NRSV)

## We Could Say Much More and Still Fall Short

Sirach 43:27–30
Ephesians 1:3–14

To hold on to hope we need an expansion of soul. We begin to look up, instead of down. We breath in, instead of out. We are surprised by delight, instead of soured by sadness. A soul that has expanded and been caught up in wonder at the beauty of nature or the astounding way God manifests his presence (cf. Sir 43:27–30) or by the deeply moving realization of what God has done for us in Christ can do nothing less than praise God who has become for him or her the All (cf. Eph 1:3–14).

> Awesome is the LORD and very great,
> and marvelous is his power. (Sir 43:29 NRSV)

> Blessed be the God and Father of our Lord Jesus Christ, who has blessed us in Christ with every spiritual blessing in the heavenly places, just as he chose us in Christ before the foundation of the world to be holy and blameless before him in love. (Eph 1:3–4 NRSV)

##  INNER HEALING

Before beginning this section you may wish to pray with the guided imagery contemplation found on page 9.

The description in Scripture of Ezekiel eating the scroll is a powerful image of how God wants to sustain us, to heal us, to strengthen us. We know that we can read Scripture passages, memorize them, repeat them, and pray with them. Sometimes, however, the question arises, "Is there something else I can do to assimilate God's word deeply into my life in order to 'eat God's word'?" Drawing on the power of image, color, and imagination I would like to suggest another method that I have found especially helpful in integrating the word of God and the affirmations that you may have formulated for yourself in the previous chapters. It is a method in which we put to use our more creative right-brain power. This process is drawing mandalas.

Mandala is a Sanskrit word meaning "sacred circle" or "finding one's center." Mandalas have been used in spirituality and in healing ministries for thousands of years. One example is the great mystic, counselor, and composer Hildegard of Bingen (1078–1179), who drew mandalas to express her visions and her beliefs about God. She is someone who sought other avenues of music, art, and nature to "eat God's words."

Making a mandala can mean simply drawing a circle (any size) and placing within it the words or phrases that we want to integrate, "to eat." The simple process of writing the words and/or phrases that have spoken deeply to us, and choosing colors and designs to accompany or illustrate them, is a way of assimilating, taking in, and digesting the words that are meaningful to us. The more we do this, the more we become like the words that God has given us and that have touched our hearts.

These mandalas, which can be drawn on individual pages or in an unlined notebook, serve as a unique and creative way of journaling. If one mandala in particular speaks to us, it can be displayed somewhere to remind us of what keeps our hope alive and who we are called to become.

Below is an illustration of what a mandala might look like.

God

I take shelter in You

I keep you before me always...

You will reveal the path of life to me...

You will give me unbounded joy in your presence

Trinity

Chapter Four

# Vitally Connected to Christ

## "My Father is the vine dresser"

 IMAGING

I have a favorite creation image of God as a gardener. The Genesis account of creation could foster the image of a God who says, "Let there be light," and—shazam!—there appears the sun in place of the darkened sky. Let there be trees. Let there be lilies. Let there be tulips. Let there be squirrels. Let there be chipmunks. Let there be grass. Let there be acorns for the squirrels to eat. With something like a magic wand we could picture God populating the earth with varieties of plants and animals.

However, my image of creation is much simpler. I picture God kneeling on the ground, a small shovel in hand, and behind him a wheelbarrow filled with tiny plants he has created. He is quietly planting the garden himself, finding just the right spot for each of his tiny plants. He knows each needs just the right amount of sun and shade. He moves quietly, communicating total peace—no goals to achieve, deadlines to meet, people to impress. God is completely at ease as he plants his garden. And I kneel next to him, my knees in the dirt, my sleeves rolled up, shovel in hand. I kneel next to God on the surface of the earth—agitated, nervous, anxious to finish before I even start. Trying to imitate, to learn; studying his method, absorbing the settled sense that surrounds him as he works.

> What a wildly wonderful world, God!
> You made it all, with Wisdom at your side,
> Made earth overflow with your wonderful creations....
> The glory of God—let it last forever!
> Let God enjoy his creation!...
> Oh, let me sing to God all my life long.
> (Ps 104:24, 31, 33 MSG)

Being in proximity with another for a length of time allows us to really know the other. It is hard to hold up the masks that hide our real self when they can see all our actions, hear our conversations, listen in on our phone calls, share the deepest feelings in our hearts—tears, smiles, anger, the works. So as I kneel next to God the Landscaper on these first days of creation, I am letting him know me as much as I am getting to know him. God surrounds himself with beauty—not only is creation beautiful, God's every movement, the peace that flows from him, is beautiful. God invites me to be beautiful—to have a beautiful spirit, to live in a lovely kindness, to pass the time in a gracious patience.

Little by little, each time I pray, I allow myself to relax a bit more in the divine Landscaper's presence, allow myself to be mentored, comforted, nurtured. Gradually, I grow in an unwavering trust in the One who gently plants the gorgeous garden of creation. As the flowers allow themselves to be planted in the garden in the place that gives God the most happiness, I learn to rest in the reality that God is good. That God is love. He wants only my happiness, and I can safely entrust to him the care of obtaining it for me.

---— ⌒⌐ —— CONTEMPLATION —— ⌐⌒—

## *"My Father is the vine dresser" (Jn 15:1 NRSV)*

Vines and branches, faithfulness and fruitfulness.... Chapter 15 of the Gospel of John with its image of a vine-dressing God reaches deep into the biblical consciousness of God's love affair with his people. The images of Israel as the vineyard of God and God's vine also appear in the Book of Isaiah and in the Psalms. They evoke themes of intimacy, joyful festivities, the broken heart of a God who suffered the infidelity of Israel (cf. Isa 5:1–7; Ps 80:8–16).

Central to New Testament ethics, however, the vine and branches are a symbol of the law of fruit bearing—Christian life is about blossoming and fruitfulness for the sake of others. This important symbol first appears in the Sermon on the Mount: a tree is judged by its fruit (cf. Mt 7:16–20). The parable of the sower comments on the different degrees of fruitfulness in those who hear the word. Some lose what they have received because they have no depth. Others are distracted. Others lose their treasure to the urgency of worldly cares. And some bear fruit thirty-, sixty-, or a hundredfold (cf. Mt 13:3–8). Toward the end of his public life, Jesus threatens to have a fig tree torn down because it has borne no fruit (cf. Lk 13:6–9). In the fifteenth chapter of John, Jesus states that the branches are judged by the fruit they produce (cf. Jn 15:1ff.). While it is clear that every Christian is to engage in fruitful activity, whence does authentic activity as a disciple originate?

Anyone who is familiar with this passage from the Gospel of John understands that Jesus is the vine and we are the branches. The Father prunes the branches so they will bear more fruit. He cuts off the barren branches and throws them away.

I used to think "pruning" meant the kind of trimming I do to my household plants. I remove a leaf here and there of a luxurious vine, leaving the plant for the most part intact. However, a visit to a vineyard one day gave me a more realistic understanding of pruning. It was early spring. I was visiting a friend and went out to the vineyard for meditation. I almost couldn't find it! The vines had been cut back to the ground. They measured only between six and sixteen inches. Only three or four shoots remained of the branches from the year before. The trellises that normally supported the vine stretched nakedly across the fields, waiting for the branches to grow long enough to bear fruit.

As Christians we like to think that we mean something, that we are making a difference in the world. We would like to be the luxuriant houseplant decorating shelves and tables, commented on, admired, attracting attention. But Jesus says we are the branches on a vine, pruned—small, dependent, hidden, not so pretty, always starting over year after year. The Christian life is meaningful according to the fruit produced. And to produce fruit we need to be vitally connected to Jesus, and to submit to being pruned by our Father. We need to give up our fruit every season. We can't gather it up in barns; hoard it; pile it up to make a show, to prove our productivity. No. Instead, each year we must begin again as a tiny bud, attached to the ancient yet ever new Vine.

Between Jesus and us there is a living and inseparably intimate relationship. The more vital our connection to the Vine, the more vibrant our following of the Master, the more we will need to be pruned. It is painful and personal, but the Father knows that only through pruning will we bear more and more fruit, year after year.

The Father prunes us through the word. What we hear in the Gospel often makes a "slit" in our heart, forcing us to realize where we haven't been faithful, where we are unfruitful, or where we are producing bad fruit. When God confronts us with his desire for our fruitfulness, the realization that we desire something else creates pain and confusion. In the struggle, the Father prunes us. Over and over again, God confronts us with the word, with a remark from a friend, with something read in a book, with an inspiration, with the good example of another, with the teaching of the Church. The more we let the Father prune us, the more fruit we will bear.

We cannot hope to be luxuriant houseplants. That is not ours to be. Instead, the Christian life progresses by detours, obstacles, confusion, struggle—and all the time the fruit is often hidden from our sight. We see the vineyard, with the tiny buds, again and again. We live in hope. In all this, we glorify God by abiding in Jesus and surrendering to the Father's vine dressing.

---

## Exploring

- Do you have a favorite image of God? What does the image represent for you? To what depths does it call you?

- When you read Scripture, do you let your imagination roam freely with the stories, the parables, the events—associating, connecting, comparing, contrasting, contemplating, observing? Would this help you to see the "life" in the word?

- What is your one-line definition of prayer?

- Have you had an exceptionally memorable experience of closeness with someone? What was it like living or being in the presence of this someone else? Did you experience changes in your heart and attitudes?

- What role does friendship play in your life? Loneliness? Family?

- Can you trust God? How might God be trying to convince you of his love and faithfulness?

- Have you noticed Christians who in their ministry bear "much fruit"? Why do you think they are so fruitful? What is the difference between fruitfulness and success? Can you talk to someone about making your ministry more fruitful?

- Jesus gave us the image of the vine and the branches to represent our complete dependence on and intimacy with him. How would you describe the way Jesus and you relate to each other? What images would you use?

- How has the Father "pruned" you? What were the circumstances? What were the feelings associated with the pruning? Were there losses? Failures? New beginnings? Surprises? Gifts?

- What is your reaction to the following lines: "We would like to be the luxuriant houseplant decorating shelves and tables, commented on, admired, attracting attention. But Jesus says we are the branches on a vine, pruned—small, dependent, hidden, not so pretty, always starting over year after year." Do you feel yourself starting over again and again? Or do you feel that your spiritual growth is a steady expansion?

- We are pruned by the Father through the word, a comment from a friend, something we read or hear, an event in our life. Is there a pattern to the way the Father prunes you? How can you surrender more fully to the Father's pruning?

## LISTENING

Take a walk outside, early in the morning or just at sunset. Walk slowly, look around you, relax, listen, absorb the sights and sounds and smells. As you become quieter within, notice what you are thinking and how you are feeling, gently holding emotions and desires and fears and dreams. You don't need to do anything more than this. Spend some time next to the Creator of the universe, slowly soaking in his presence in the midst of the beautiful garden he has planted just for you.

## Resting

Resting with these passages of Scripture can deepen your healing. To prepare yourself to rest deeply in your heart where healing can truly take place, you can repeat the listening prayer experience above before you use any of these Scripture passages, or you can place yourself in the scene described in the passage. Each time tell Jesus what you see and what you feel, and wait for him to say something to you.

### Being Present to One Another

Ruth 1:8–17
Luke 1:35–45

Unexpectedly, two women were lifted out of obscurity, called to play particularly important roles in salvation history. Ruth, a Moabite woman, married the Israelite Boaz and became the grandmother of King David. Mary, a virgin, was overshadowed by the Spirit and became the mother of the Son of God. Both women also were intimately bound up in the lives of others. Ruth leaves her pagan home in the valley of Moab to accompany and care for her mother-in-law, Naomi. "Wherever you go, I will go too," she tells her (cf. Ruth 1:8–17). Mary rushes off at the angel's hint and spent several months caring for her elderly cousin Elizabeth who also, unexpectedly and miraculously, is with child (cf. Lk 1:35–45). Both women allow themselves to be present to another, accepting the vulnerability of others' presence and giving themselves over to God's presence and plan.

Ruth to her mother-in-law:

> "Do not press me to leave you
> or to turn back from following you!
> Where you go, I will go;
> where you lodge, I will lodge;
> your people shall be my people,
> and your God my God." (Ruth 1:16 NRSV)

Mary's visit to Elizabeth:

> When Elizabeth heard Mary's greeting, the child leapt in her womb. And Elizabeth was filled with the Holy Spirit and exclaimed with a loud cry, "Blessed are you among women, and blessed is the fruit of your womb. And why has this happened to me, that the mother of my Lord comes to me? For as soon as I heard the sound of your greeting, the child in my womb leapt for joy. And blessed is she who believed that there would be a fulfillment of what was spoken to her by the Lord." (Lk 1:41–45 NRSV)

## God's Love Affair with Us

Zephaniah 3:16–20
John 13:1–5

The relationship between God and Israel throughout the Old Testament is alternately tender and volatile as God woos his chosen people to a complete trust and absolute fidelity (cf. Zeph 3:16–20). At one point Jesus speaks strongly with Peter, who had counseled him to forget Jerusalem and the cross. Another time Jesus gently encourages Peter to allow him to wash his feet (cf. Jn 13:1–5). At one moment the Scriptures are bursting forth in ecstatic promises of God's restorative justice. At another moment the pages intimate the secrets of this God who became one of us to restore us to love through his own life, sorrowful death, and glorious resurrection. The same tension and power of these emotions are played out in our own relationship with the Lord.

God's relationship with Israel:

> The LORD, your God, is in your midst,
> a warrior who gives victory;
> he will rejoice over you with gladness,
> he will renew you in his love;
> he will exult over you with loud singing
> as on a day of festival.
> I will remove disaster from you,
> so that you will not bear reproach for it.
> (Zeph 3:17–18 NRSV)

Jesus kneels to wash Peter's feet:

> And during supper Jesus, knowing that the Father had given all things into his hands, and that he had come from God and was going to God, got up from the table, took off his outer robe, and tied a towel around himself. Then he poured water into a basin and began to wash the disciples' feet and to wipe them with the towel that was tied around him. (Jn 13:2–5 NRSV)

## You Are Still Living by Your Natural Inclinations

Acts 9:1–9

1 Corinthians 3:1–4

The biblical term "pruning," which would have been so clear to the agrarian Israelite culture, could also be expressed, in today's parlance, as transforming, maturing, renewing, or converting. Paul had a major pruning experience at the beginning of his following of Christ. The story of Paul's encounter with Christ

on the road to Damascus is well known. Paul, then known as
Saul, was a Pharisee, in every way an upright and righteous Jew.
But pride, arrogance, careerism, and self-reliance were pruned
that day as he was led by the hand into Damascus, the city he had
come to invade with his violent intentions to search out and
imprison followers of Jesus (cf. Acts 9:1–9). It was a drastic pruning. In his turn, however, when he became the Apostle to the
Gentiles, bringing many to belief in the Lord Jesus, he assisted
the Divine Gardener with his pruning. Letters, tears, arguments,
explanations, tender compassion, and fierce loyalty all were
brought to bear on the desire that these new followers of Jesus
would be people who lived of the Spirit, mature Christians
capable of "solid food," not just milk. As Jesus had been clear and
direct with him, Paul was not afraid to clearly point out what
needed to be discarded for them to be entirely renewed in Christ
(cf. 1 Cor 3:1–4).

Paul's pruning experience:

> Now as he was going along and approaching Damascus, sud-
> denly a light from heaven flashed around him. He fell to the
> ground and heard a voice saying to him, "Saul, Saul, why do
> you persecute me?" He asked, "Who are you, Lord?" The reply
> came, "I am Jesus, whom you are persecuting. But get up and
> enter the city, and you will be told what you are to do." (Acts
> 9:3–6 NRSV)

Paul's letters to the Christian communities:

> I fed you with milk, not solid food, for you were not ready for
> solid food. Even now you are still not ready, for you are still of
> the flesh. For as long as there is jealousy and quarreling among
> you, are you not of the flesh, and behaving according to
> human inclinations? (1 Cor 3:2–3 NRSV)

## ꧁— Inner Healing —꧂

Before beginning this section you may wish to pray with the guided imagery contemplation found on page 9.

To be "pruned" is to have taken from us what we relied upon, what we loved, what contributed to our sense of identity. Pruning can touch our careers, our finances, our families, our friends, our health, and more. Pruning brings us to let go of aspects of these things that are, in the metaphor of vineyard and pruning, so many leaves and branches and cherished fruits in our lives. Yet, the secret in living through pruning times in our lives also lies precisely in the image of the vine. Just as a vine is more than its fruit and its leaves, we also are more than the work we do, the relationships we have, our volunteer ministries, or our titles.

For us, pruning is usually associated with loss, and loss is to a greater or lesser degree painful. Every loss offers us an invitation to learn something about ourselves. It is a call to grow, to discover aspects of ourselves of which we were not aware. Every loss, while not necessarily willed by God, is permitted by God, and offers us a blessing which we can only claim after a time of grieving and letting go. There is a blessing hidden in every experience of loss that may take a long time to claim, but it is there if we have the eyes to see. The Sufi mystic Rumi said it well: "Don't get lost in your pain, / know that one day / your pain will become your cure."[2]

Take some time to look back on your life. Make a list of your losses. For every experience of loss, ask God to help you claim the blessings that came from it. Perhaps you became more compassionate or more understanding. Maybe you discovered hidden

---

2. Rumi, *Hidden Music,* Azima Melita Kolin and Maryam Mafi translators (San Francisco: HarperElement, 2001), 136.

strength. The loss may have helped you to deepen your experience of God. Perhaps new people came into your life. You may have simplified your lifestyle and grown in gratitude for the blessings of each day. It could be that you recognized that you had to reclaim parts of yourself that you had buried deep within.

Take some time to thank God, not so much for the losses, but for the blessings that came from the losses. Ask God to help you claim more of your inner strength, to have the courage to look not only at the pain, but also to see the light beyond it.

If you are finding it difficult to let go of the losses, ritualize letting them go. One helpful way is to find small rocks and on each of them to write a word that represents a loss associated with the time of your pruning with which you are struggling. Put these in a bag and carry them around for a few days. You will find it quite annoying to carry this added weight. This is a good metaphor for the inner baggage you continue to carry. When you are ready, take the rocks to a quiet place and hand each one over to God, asking God to help you let go. You can then bury them or throw them into an empty field or into a river. Pray for the grace to forgive those people or situations involved in the loss you experienced.

Chapter Five

# A Future Only God
# Could Dream Of

*"Take Mary to be your wife"*

 IMAGING

Last year I had an important decision to make. My choice
would affect not only the direction of my own life, but the lives
of others as well. It was a decision that was not entirely up to me
to make, and yet it depended entirely on my response. It was during the months when I was reflecting on this decision that I had
the following image in prayer.

I was finding it hard to surrender myself wholly to God in
prayer. I was worried. I wanted to figure out what could be the
outcome of the two possible choices before me. I was calculating
what I thought would be the wisest move. With all this mental
activity going on, I couldn't pray. One morning I asked Jesus just
to come to me. I closed my eyes and pictured myself near a very
large lake. I imagined Jesus coming to me. Usually Jesus comes
to me on foot. This time, however, he came by boat. In a little
rowboat he drew up to the edge of the dock and invited me to sit

beside him. I dropped down into the rowboat from the dock, settled myself, and looked at Jesus. He was hoping for some leisurely time together. Instead I tried to grab the oars from him and efficiently set my sights on the other side of the lake. He handed the oars over and said, "Okay now, go ahead and row to the other side." I positioned myself and began to row and we started moving in circles. Splashing and pulling and stretching I tried to reposition myself again and again in an attempt to start moving toward the other shore. No matter what I tried, we moved no more than a few yards from the dock.

I was embarrassed and frustrated. It became clear to me from that image that my rowing—my trying to figure out what I should do—was getting me nowhere. I was literally turning around in circles. Instead of analysis, I needed receptivity. Instead of control, I needed vulnerability; instead of plans, trust.

Holding on to hope demands this transition from the small circular world that we are able to create—a world that forever circles around ourselves—to the movement of a follower along a road that is straight and narrow. Any growth in spirituality requires this biblical transformation. This was made clear from the very first breaths of Jesus' public life. Plunging into the River Jordan, Jesus faces his cousin. With others milling around the edge of the lake, John the Baptist looks deeply into Jesus' eyes and sees someone different—the voice, the word, the light, the way, the truth, the life—and he shrinks back. You can just hear him thinking, "Whoa! Now what do I do? The one who is coming after me is here. What is he doing asking for baptism? He shouldn't need baptism! Not my baptism. What is supposed to happen next? What would happen if I didn't say anything and just baptized him? After all, he didn't announce himself. Or should I bow down? Or should I say something?"

"I should be baptized by you," John blurts out. John is trying to figure it out. To plan. To do it right. To do what makes sense.

Jesus' response is straightforward, "Just fulfill the plan for now. Go ahead and do what is right here before you. Baptize me, my cousin. Don't try to orchestrate the coming of the kingdom."

After John, trembling, baptizes his Messiah and Jesus steps out of the River Jordan, the Spirit descends upon Jesus and the Father proclaims him his Son, inviting the world to listen to him (cf. Mt 3:13–17).

Trying to figure things out invites circular, self-propelled thinking that in the end goes nowhere. Obedience, openness, and discipleship invite the Spirit into our lives to reveal to us who we are and who Jesus is.

## CONTEMPLATION

### *"Take Mary to be your wife" (Mt 1:20 NRSV)*

The Scriptures are full of God telling people what to do. Some people cast their lot on God and follow his lead. Others run the other direction. Some ignore him, others forget him, a few hate him. These stories become the living context of our own lives as we also stand before the lasting meaning of life—our life in particular.

Jonah, the prophet, and Joseph, the foster father of Jesus, are larger-than-life figures that often help me get my bearings before God, to evaluate my stance before the God who calls.

Jonah had it figured out. "Now the word of the LORD came to Jonah son of Amittai, saying, 'Go at once to Nineveh, that great city, and cry out against it; for their wickedness has come up before me'" (Jon 1:1–2). Jonah probably started thinking, "This is not good. Nineveh is the capital of Assyria, the Ninevites are a violent people. Why does God care about them? I'm likely to get myself killed. And besides that, I'm no fool! I'm going to go there and announce the judgment of God, they're going to say they are sorry, and God is going to forgive them. Forgive the enemies of Israel! Show them the same love and mercy he shows us! They should all be wiped out. What interest does God have in them? I will not go!" In fact, near the end of the short book of Jonah, he tells God exactly that: He yells at God, "God! I knew it—when I was back home, I knew that was going to happen! . . . I knew you were sheer grace and mercy, not easily angered, rich in love, and ready at the drop of a hat to turn your plans of punishment into a program of forgiveness!" (Jon 4:1–2 MSG)

And so Jonah gets on a ship and goes the other direction. God has to really go out of his way to drag Jonah back to Nineveh to carry out the mission he had given this self-propelled prophet. Jonah can't recognize his mission. He can't hear the voice of his God. He wants things his own way. Jonah's choices lead to regrets: Experiencing storms on the high seas that put his fellow travelers at risk, being tossed overboard, having to retrace his steps to do what he had been sent to do, and eventually sulking over God's goodness and compassion. His life becomes a string of regrets. He is morose, bitter, and vengeful, as the final conversation between him and God reveals. "What have you to be angry at?" God asks. Jonah leaves the city and sulks. God arranges for a plant to cool him, which makes Jonah happy. By dawn a worm has destroyed the plant, which makes Jonah furious. "I'm better off dead!" he shouts at God, waving his fist in the direction of the Almighty. Then God asks Jonah why he thinks it was all right for him to change his feelings from pleasure to anger overnight over a mere plant, and begrudge God a change of heart from anger to pleasure over an entire city that has repented of wickedness and turned to him in hope (cf. Jon 4:9–11).

The book ends with no response from Jonah. One wonders if he ever got over himself. His circular thinking certainly didn't make for a pleasant life.

Joseph, on the other hand, also finds himself called by God into an unpleasant situation. His betrothed, his beloved Mary, is obviously with child, but not his own. He had trusted her. She seems to have betrayed his love. His plans for the future crumble at the heartbreaking realization that she was not what he had believed her to be. But being a good man, Joseph tries to figure out what to do. He still loves her. He doesn't want her to be hurt. Legally he should have her publicly stoned to death. He wants to do the right thing. But he wants to protect her also. He looks outside of himself and his hurt and his plans—outside the circle of his self-interest—and opens up a hole in his sorrow for the grace of God to construct a future beyond human calculation.

"Take Mary to be your wife" (cf. Mt 1:20). Her child is of the Holy Spirit. You are to take care of them. You are to give him his name.

God doesn't usually reveal futures, he simply points out the next step—and that often makes absolutely no sense. Joseph doesn't run the other way. He is warned, "Get out of town; Herod is looking for the child to kill him." Seven years later, "Go back to Israel now, it's safe." When they get into Israelite territory, another warning, "Don't go to Judah, go to the hills of Galilee; go to Nazareth." That's it. And Joseph obeys.

Joseph followed the plan of God and gave up relying solely on his own ability to figure out the best for himself and his family. His choices led to wholeness. As with Jonah, the plan of God put the person in second place. Jonah refused to be "second in command" and follow the directives of the Captain. He refused to place himself as servant to the Ninevites, to live for others. Joseph's call meant that instead of having the highest dignity in this family, he had the vulnerable position of looking out for the two central figures in the history of salvation: Jesus and Mary. He was their support. He followed God's instructions and provided for his family. Because of his gentleness, he was able to engage the suffering he encountered in taking Mary as his wife, to protect the Child Jesus from Herod, to live as an exile, to return to Israel, to live and die in obscurity without one recorded word of his own in the Scriptures.

Joseph moved toward what threatened him. In this courageous act, he took up the mission God had assigned; in the very obedience laid upon him, he was revealed to himself and he came to know the inner heart of God. God takes the initiative to lay out a plan for us, an action to take, a journey upon which to embark, and in leaving the circle of our small fears and plans for our lives, we discover a future only God could dream of.

## EXPLORING

- Can you remember a decision you had to make that was decisive for your own future and that affected others? What did you feel as you prepared to make the decision? Anxiety? Anticipation? Responsibility? Paralysis? Trust?

- Does the image of the rowboat resonate with you? What does it remind you of? How have you gotten beyond a pattern of thinking or acting that was getting you nowhere?

- Do you tend to try to figure things out, or do you have another way of approaching your problems or decisions? Can you talk about an experience in which you had to give up figuring things out and just trust? What happened?

- Has God ever told you what to do? What were the circumstances? Was your response more like Jonah's or Joseph's? What would you need to do in order to hear God's voice more clearly?

- How do your choices lead to wholeness?

- Can you describe a time you ran away from God?

- Do you think God asks us to do things beyond our strength? Referring to both the story of Jonah and Joseph, what are some reasons that these plans of God seem so hard?

- When your dreams have been disappointed, as Joseph's were, what did you do? Did God show you a way through the ruins of your plans?

- Are you growing in your ability to leave the circle of your fears and plans and embark on a future only God could dream of?

## LISTENING

Close your eyes and picture yourself at the side of a large lake. Is it day or night? Is the sun or the moon reflected in the waters? Is the lake calm or choppy? What do you hear around you? What do you see around you? Is anyone else near you? As you stand there, let significant events from the past day or week rise to the surface of your awareness along with the emotions attached to them. Let yourself feel these events reverberate within your consciousness. From the left side a small boat slowly approaches, pausing, rocking gently on the waters. You realize it is Jesus coming to you, asking you if you'd like to come with him. What happens next?

## RESTING

Resting with these passages of Scripture can deepen your healing. To prepare yourself to rest deeply in your heart where healing can truly take place, you can repeat the listening prayer experience above before you use any of these Scripture passages, or you can place yourself into the scene described in the passage. Each time tell Jesus what you see and what you feel, and wait for him to say something to you.

### When We Can't Figure It Out

> John 2:1–12
> John 19:25–27

In two passages of John's Gospel Mary steps in to save people from spinning their wheels fruitlessly as they try to solve a problem. The first is at the wedding celebration at Cana, a festive neighborhood party that lasts several days. As the wine begins to run out, Mary sees the problem. Instead of fretting, figuring out how to buy more, coming up with excuses for the bride and groom to offer, or trying to escape the coming catastrophe, she goes straight to Jesus and tells him the problem (cf. Jn 2:1–12). At the end of Jesus' life, as she watches her son die a humiliated failure, she accepts her role as mother of the apostles, who are devastated by the latest turn of events. They certainly would not have known how to go on. They had already figured out that they had better lie low or they would be next to be executed, hardly a promising beginning to the Kingdom of God. Nevertheless, in the darkest chaos, when Jesus' ministry seems to be blacking out, she holds a candle to light the way. She steps in to show the apostles they don't need to work on solving a problem (cf. Jn 19:25–27).

When the wine gave out, the mother of Jesus said to him, "They have no wine." And Jesus said to her, "Woman, what concern is that to you and to me? My hour has not yet come." His mother said to the servants, "Do whatever he tells you." (Jn 2:3–4 NRSV)

When Jesus saw his mother and the disciple whom he loved standing beside her, he said to his mother, "Woman, here is your son." (Jn 19:26 NRSV)

## Don't Send Me

Ezekiel 3:14–27
Jeremiah 1:4–10

Jonah is not alone in the Scriptures as a reluctant prophet. Others have hesitated at or suffered because of the mission they have been chosen for. Ezekiel's prophetic mission bridged the great disaster of 586 B.C., when Jerusalem was completely destroyed by the Babylonians and its population exiled. The glory of God appeared to him and called him to face off the denial and despair of his people with the memory of God's love and fidelity. God told him that it was going to be hard work and that probably no one in the rebellious house of Israel would listen to him. Chapter 3 states that the Spirit lifted him up and took him away. When he came to the exiles he sat there among them, stunned, for seven days (cf. Ezek 3:14–27). On the other end of the spectrum is Jeremiah, the youthful prophet, who said, "But I am too young." To this God responded simply: "Do not say you are too young. I will tell you where to go and what to say" (cf. Jer 1:4–10).

Call of Ezekiel:

Then the hand of the LORD was upon me there; and he said to me, "Rise up, go out into the valley, and there I will speak with you." So I rose up and went out into the valley; and the glory of the LORD stood there, like the glory that I had seen by the

river Chebar.... The spirit entered into me, and set me on my
feet; and he spoke with me. (Ezek 3:22–23, 24 NRSV)

Call of Jeremiah:

Then the LORD put out his hand and touched my mouth; and
the LORD said to me,
"Now I have put my words in your mouth.
See, today I appoint you over nations and over kingdoms,
to pluck up and to pull down,
to destroy and to overthrow,
to build and to plant." (Jer 1:9–10 NRSV)

## Only the Next Step

Judges 6:11–7:25
Acts 8:26–40

When God calls a person to a specific mission he gives them
the overall picture and then tells them only what they should do
next. It would certainly be reassuring if we knew what would
happen after we take the next step. Often the next step doesn't
seem to have anything to do with the overall vision. Always the
next step puts us either at the service of, or in submission to, the
community. When God called Gideon, he told him to go and
deliver Israel from the power of the Midians. "I hereby commis-
sion you" (cf. Judg 6:14). He didn't elaborate a strategy. In fact,
God thinned out the ranks of his "soldiers," doing everything
possible to make it impossible to create an effective strategy.
Gideon was at the service of the community on God's terms, and
through him God was serving and saving the community (cf.
Judg 6:11–7:25). An angel of the Lord gave Philip a mission: "Go
to the road that goes south from Jerusalem to Gaza." Then when
he got there, "You see that chariot over there. Catch up to it and
ask the driver if you can join him." Hardly an impressive mission
(cf. Acts 8:26–40). But all authentic missions begin with one step,

taken in the dark, at the command of the Lord. And it is clear who is in charge. If these conditions are not there, then you need to examine if you yourself are the source of your mission.

Call of Gideon:

> The LORD said to Gideon, "The troops with you are too many for me to give the Midianites into their hand. Israel would only take the credit away from me, saying, 'My own hand has delivered me.' Now therefore proclaim this in the hearing of the troops, 'Whoever is fearful and trembling, let him return home.'" (Judg 7:2–3 NRSV)

Mission of Philip:

> The eunuch asked Philip, "About whom, may I ask you, does the prophet say this, about himself or about someone else?" Then Philip began to speak, and starting with this scripture, he proclaimed to him the good news about Jesus. As they were going along the road, they came to some water; and the eunuch said, "Look, here is water! What is to prevent me from being baptized?" (Acts 8:34–36 NRSV)

## INNER HEALING

Before beginning this section you may wish to pray with the guided imagery contemplation found on page 9.

Many of the people called by God experience, in the face of this vocation, mixed emotions and a great deal of fear. There is a psychological principle that in the absence of facts, of real information, our imaginations take over and we expect the worst. We find ourselves worrying about all the ways that something could go wrong.

There are many biblical stories that illustrate this initial tendency. Joseph thinks he will have to divorce Mary; Jonah decides to run away; Esther initially tries to withdraw from the impending tragedy of her people; Jeremiah claims he is too young and cannot do what God is asking of him. Each of these people and everyone else called by God is asked to take a risk and to trust God's guidance.

We too are called by God to be God's presence in the world and to make choices that are in line with Gospel values. Yet, we often find ourselves worrying about what the outcome of our choices might be. According to certain studies, 40 percent of what we worry about will never happen and 30 percent is about things that happened in the past over which we have no control. How much energy is wasted!

One helpful tool toward greater peace is the creation of a "worry box" (or, instead of a box, it could be a bag or journal). When you find yourself stuck and unable to move forward because of constant worries, write your concerns on a piece of paper and slip it into the worry box. In doing this, you are ritualizing your desire to hand over to God your unproductive habit of worrying. Whenever the thought comes up again, remember that you have placed the concern in God's hands and reframe your anxious thoughts into a prayer. For example, if you are worried about a trip you must make or an interview that is coming up, let your prayer be a positive act of trust: "I trust, O God, that all shall be well" or, "I am confidant, O God, that you are always with me."

Every four or five months, read through all the papers placed in the box. Notice how many of the concerns that created your worries never actually happened. Discard those papers. Put back in the box the concerns you still have, and add any new ones that come up. Continue to pray to God with trust, placing your worries in God's hands.

Chapter Six

# Throw Your Arms Around Jesus

## *"Become like the youngest"*

 IMAGING

It wasn't a dream. There it was on my computer screen: Bold, red letters in 32-point type accusing me of trying to ruin someone's project. What's going to happen to me? flashed through my mind, barely registering on my consciousness. Deeper, hidden completely, only realized later, was the inner frustration of not measuring up to an image of what I thought I should be. When I allowed myself to touch the fear that I usually fled from, I finally recognized the violent aggression I directed at myself— the self-hatred. So foolish, I thought.

I often fantasized that I was someone different, somewhere different, somehow different because I hated who I was. I was afraid to live life—my life—just as it was, just who I was. But how foolish. It is only in the embracing of one's real self that one will find true peace. Compared to our fantasies of ourselves, our reality seems too small, too susceptible to the ebb and flow of the tides of life. However, as one spiritual director said to me, "It seems small because it's real."

So I asked Jesus to say something to me as I read the angry e-mail. I expected comfort and solace from him. Instead in prayer he took me outside and said simply, "This is the way it is."

The way it is. The way life is. There are highs and lows. There is excitement and sadness. There is success and failure. There is exhilaration and disorientation. This is the way it is.

We cannot escape the waves of consolation and desolation that wash through our souls. Nor can we avoid the euphoric moods and the dark depressions that with a gentle or harsh rhythm seem to pull us on a leash.

Those of us who have struggled in our lives with emotional chaos and inner turmoil might find ourselves tricked into thinking that having survived the swirling darkness we should now stay in the land of light. The ups and downs will smooth out into one continuous upward journey. We may feel terrified of another bout with darkness. The internal stress we create for ourselves by fleeing the rhythm of life makes us shallow people. We need to be able to dip back into the darkness here and there with graciousness and without fear in order to learn to relax there, where God is also present.

## CONTEMPLATION

### *"Become like the youngest" (Lk 22:26 NRSV)*

In one of the rooms of our convent there is a large picture of Jesus at the Last Supper. The image depicts the moments following Jesus' statement that one of the apostles was about to betray him. Jesus is surrounded by three of his close followers. Two of them, one certainly Peter, stand in the shadows behind Jesus, looming over him, wanting to know who would do such a thing.

Perhaps they want to do everything they can to prevent it from happening. Perhaps they want to make sure it won't be them. After all, such a tragedy would mean the end of their life with Jesus as they knew it. In the foreground, the third apostle, John, the one whom Jesus loved, lays his head on Jesus' heart, his arms around his neck, in a gesture of listening and entrustment. His face is quiet. He will not let go. The figures of Jesus and he are in the light, and a sense of peace pervades them. The Gospel of John says simply that John, at the direction of Peter, asks Jesus who it is who would betray him. Jesus tells the young apostle simply that it is the one who would dip his hand into the dish with him. Then he turns to Judas and says, "Go and do what you must do. Do it quickly!" And from the peaceful upper room where they enjoyed the Passover together, Jesus and his followers are thrust into the darkness. It is night. There is no evasion of reality, only a quiet acceptance of the rhythm of life.

When darkness or failure or loss threatens, I am often like Peter: "Tell me how it is going to happen and I will get rid of the precipitating event. Let's keep everything the way it was." The beloved disciple instead puts his head on Jesus' heart and asks to know how it is to happen that he might be inseparable from his Lord and teacher. Peter takes command. John takes cover in the arms of the one who just moments before had washed his feet with the utmost discretion and humility.

The motif of the Beloved Disciple, the one whom Jesus loved, surfaces precisely before this imminent plunge into the darkness, in the midst of the rising anxiety that threatens to cut the apostles off from trust in the ultimate victory of their Messiah. The Beloved Disciple, in the face of this, chooses not to escape, but to cling to Jesus, to remain "with," to refuse to go it alone.

The Gospel of John exposes the futility of our efforts to evade reality by trying to bend it to our benefit. The author brings this home to us through each conversation he records in its pages. Every question or statement that is directed to Jesus in this Gospel misses the mark. The word remains above and beyond the reach of our puny minds. For example, Nicodemus asks incredulously, "How can you say that? That doesn't make sense to say we must be born again. Can people who are already adults be born again?" (cf. Jn 3:4).

The Samaritan woman listens carefully to a strange man sitting at the well of her town, a man who promises her that if she drinks the living water he would give her she will never thirst again: "That's fantastic. I could save a lot of time if I didn't have to come to this well daily for water. Give me some of that water, so that I may never be thirsty again" (cf. Jn 4:15). Philip rebukes Jesus, who wants to feed the crowds who had been listening to his preaching and are now hungry: "Are you kidding? Two hundred denarii would not buy enough to give them a little piece each. Where are we going to get the money for this great banquet you want to throw?" (cf. Jn 6:7).

John alone, in the ups and downs of life, shows us how to relate to Jesus, the Word made flesh, and it is not with many words. It is with love. Casting his arms around Jesus he lays his head on his Master's heart. He later follows Jesus through the night of his capture and trial by the Sanhedrin. He stands by Mary beneath the cross, uttering no words. We only hear his words written later in his letters:

> "My dear friends,
> let us love each other,
> since love is from God." (1 Jn 4:7 NJB)

John had learned from Jesus that in life the only important thing is love. And we must be small to love. If we are too big, we fight, compete, evade, rationalize, escape. But if we remain as a child, as Jesus remained a child before the Father, we hand ourselves over to God, and even in the face of darkness and hatred we love. Love is the ultimate word. It was the Father's final Word—Jesus. It must eventually become our only word. With this assurance of love and safety we can be confident of finding Jesus even in the places of darkness in our lives. We can relax enough to discover meaning in everything that happens to us. Love can open our eyes to recognize the resurrection that always follows death, the dawn that follows the night, the consolation that follows disorienting desolation.

## EXPLORING

- Can you remember a time of deep disappointment? What was the precipitating event? What were the feelings? Were you able to take time to process what was happening?

- What happens when you take time out after an unexpected upset? Have you ever just remained quietly still for a few moments? For hours? For days? What did you learn?

- What changes when you become present to how you are feeling? What changes in the way you approach events when you become present to the unfolding of your inner world?

- How have you experienced the rhythm of life? Trace an autobiographical sketch of the ups and downs of your life.

- How do you feel about darkness in your life?

- If you have struggled with depression before, do you have fears about your depression returning? What are they? Have you had experiences in which you have felt your life deepened through the experience of disappointment or melancholy?

- Have you ever tried to prevent something from happening out of fear? Did it work? For how long?

- Do you feel more like Peter or like John in your approach to dark or frightful events? How have you lived this out? What changes would you want to make?

- What does this mean to you: "John alone shows us how to relate to Jesus, the Word made flesh, in the ups and downs of life . . . and it is not with words. It is with love"? What could God be asking you?

- When you hear that you must be little, like a child, how do you react? What are your fears or your desires?

- Have you ever tried to reason with God why something shouldn't be happening? What was the result? Would there have been a better way to live through this reality?

## LISTENING

Picture yourself in the midst of the apostles at the Last Supper. Judas has just left the room. You aren't sure where he is going or why. Some of the apostles are discussing among themselves what they think is going on. Peter is protesting that he will follow Jesus even if he should have to die for him. Jesus seems sad. There is an air of uncertainty. Then John takes you by the hand, leads you to the seat next to Jesus, and tells you to put your arms around Jesus and lay your head on his heart. Stay here for as long as you need to in order to hear the words Jesus will say to you.

## RESTING

Resting with these passages of Scripture can deepen your healing. To prepare yourself to rest deeply in your heart where healing can truly take place, you can repeat the listening prayer experience above before you use any of these Scripture passages, or you can place yourself into the scene described in the passage. Each time tell Jesus what you see and what you feel, and wait for him to say something to you.

## Poverty of Spirit

Luke 19:41–44
1 Corinthians 4:14–16

In the Scriptures, tears are often the outward sign of encountering poverty, one's inability to control others, misunderstanding, and rejection. Jesus wept over Jerusalem shortly before his death. How he had longed to draw the people into the dynamic life of love he enjoyed with the Father, but they could not hear the passion of his heart because their own hearts were deafened by judgments, biases, and assumptions (cf. Lk 19:41–44). Saint Paul struggled terribly with the community at Corinth. These new converts in the wild port city of Corinth had grown into a community in Christ during the year and a half that Paul had stayed among them. But in his absence factions developed, immoral behavior appeared, and worship was usurped by self-centeredness. Paul wrote with tears to this community, going over the same ground again and again, that they might be rooted and built up in Christ (cf. 1 Cor 4:14–16).

> As he came near and saw the city, he wept over it, saying, "If you, even you, had only recognized on this day the things that make for peace!" (Lk 19:41 NRSV)

> For though you might have ten thousand guardians in Christ, you do not have many fathers. Indeed, in Christ Jesus I became your father through the gospel. (1 Cor 4:15 NRSV)

## *Intimacy in Times When We Feel Threatened and Afraid*

> Luke 8:22–25
> John 8:1–11

When we are in need we usually remember God exists and probably could do something to help. A bumper sticker I saw recently stated truthfully: "As long as there are exams, there will be prayer in schools." We send up a prayer to the heavens for help. When the disciples were tossed about in the sudden squall on the Lake of Galilee, they awoke Jesus with the statement: Don't you realize we are going to drown? Jesus stood up and calmed the lake. Jesus helped them to experience his power when they seemed at nature's mercy (cf. Lk 8:22–25). To the woman suffering the public humiliation of the accusation of adultery, Jesus offered protection from shame. Jesus put himself on her level, bending down and writing in the dust. It was an intimate conversation between the sinner and the Savior (cf. Jn 8:1–11).

> "Master, Master, we are perishing!" And he woke up and rebuked the wind and the raging waves; they ceased, and there was calm. (Lk 8:24–25 NRSV)

> "Teacher, this woman was caught in the very act of committing adultery. . . ." Jesus bent down and wrote with his finger on the ground. (Jn 8:4, 6 NRSV)

## *When Things Don't Work Out*

> 1 Kings 19:1–18
> John 19:25–30

For holy people, prophets, followers of Jesus, obedient disciples of the Lord, things don't always work out. In fact, they didn't work out for Jesus. When the tide has turned against us, it is helpful to take refuge in the accounts of those who have sought the face of the Almighty in the midst of the storm. Elijah is a good example. This prophet of Yahweh had shut up the heavens bringing drought to the land and called down fire from heaven in his contest with the prophets of Baal. He had brought the dead back to life and had sent kings down to destruction, depriving them of power and prestige (cf. Sir 48:1–11). However, pursued by the murderous Jezebel, he flees to the desert, saying, "I have had it. I am no better than anyone else." An angel appears to him and gives him food and drink to journey to Horeb. There God speaks intimately with him in a tiny whispering sound, giving him direction (cf. 1 Kings 19:1–18).

Mary is another example. She, as any mother, had stood by her child through his entire life. She knows who Jesus is, for Gabriel the angel has told her. Yet she has to stand by helplessly as he is misunderstood, ridiculed, persecuted, and then finally put to death. As she stood beneath the cross, what must have passed through her mind? Doubt? This certainly wasn't the throne of Israel the angel had promised. Fear? What would become of the tiny movement he had started? It was so small, so new, so fragile. Anger? How could they do this to my beautiful son! (cf. Jn 19:25–30).

Elijah:

> "It is enough; now, O LORD, take away my life, for I am no better than my ancestors." Then he lay down under the broom tree and fell asleep. Suddenly an angel touched him and said to him, "Get up and eat." He looked, and there at his head was a cake baked on hot stones, and a jar of water. He ate and drank, and lay down again. The angel of the LORD came a second time, touched him, and said, "Get up and eat, otherwise the journey will be too much for you." (1 Kings 19:4–7 NRSV)

Mary beneath the cross:

> Meanwhile, standing near the cross of Jesus were his mother,
> and his mother's sister, Mary the wife of Clopas, and Mary
> Magdalene. (Jn 19:25 NRSV)

## INNER HEALING

Before beginning this section you may wish to pray with the
guided imagery contemplation found on page 9.

Fear, panic, and anxiety touch each of us at certain times in
our lives. For some people these emotions are especially frighten-
ing because they open the door to a place of great darkness. It is
no wonder the words "be not afraid" and "fear not" are written
365 times in Scripture. In our fragile human existence, we need
daily confirmations of God's presence and provident care.

God is indeed present in every cell of our body and is as close
to us as our very breath. Breathing is as essential to spiritual life
as it is to physical life. When we panic, we forget to breathe. And
so, one way of reminding ourselves that we are always in the
presence of the Holy One is to stop, breathe, and listen.

Stop whatever you are doing and put a halt to the chatter in
your mind.

Breathe deeply. Close your mouth and inhale deeply through
your nose, counting from one to four. Exhale slowly, counting
from one to six. You should feel your stomach moving out and
then in with each breath. After a slight pause, repeat the same
process, focusing on your breath. Sink into the silence created by
each pause between breaths.

Listen to the voice of Holy Wisdom from deep within you.

When you begin to feel the calmness settling into your body,
you may want to pray a simple prayer. Any prayer or word will

do, but you may find the words below comforting. They may be prayed for yourself or for someone else:

> May I be held safe in the arms of God.
> May I be open to God's guiding presence.
> May I be an instrument of peace at all times.

Chapter Seven

# Getting Your Inside World Put Right

## *"Blessed are the pure in heart"*

 IMAGING

Images can be rich sources of inspiration; they also can directly confront our values and behavior with the call of the Gospel. A recent image that came to me as I asked God to show me where I needed conversion was just such a confrontation. In the image I was on a pilgrimage, walking through a lush countryside, approaching a large city that seemed to pop out of the valley unexpectedly. It was dusk as I left the flowers and birds behind and drew nearer to what seemed to be a dusty, overpopulated, polluted place. I walked along, watching the lights in the windows switch on, one after the other, as the streets began to empty of snarled traffic and overcrowded sidewalks. A friend appeared beside me and, before walking on, said only one sentence: "In this city you will find a guide."

In the city, I looked around expectantly for this guide as I ventured down a main street. Instead of continuing toward the office buildings that reached their arms high into the sky, however, I found myself turning down a back alley. At the other end of the alley I took a right and then a quick left down another small side street strewn with trash bins and garbage, and then immediately found myself under a large bridge where people had built fires for light and warmth. This was "home" for a large crowd who met here each evening, having nowhere else to go, not belonging to the society that lived in the high-rises that stretched to the heavens.

That is where I found her, my guide. She was combing her long, blond frizzy hair, which fell quietly over the clean, simple clothes she wore. Flowers graced her hair; a point of beauty in the obvious poverty around her. This wisdom figure turned to me and said: "You have lived by the values of the big city. Here we live by simple beauties and total dependence. No getting ahead. Long nights with nothing to eat or read. No 'to do' lists to check off."

"I have wasted my life," I blurted out, surprising even myself, for she had touched some reservoir of desire deep within me.

Smiling, she responded, "It's not too late to make the vow to live with the poor, to be totally dependent, to be beautiful, and to create beauty."

"If I do that, I will disappear. I am afraid—no status, no address, no memory of me, no place in the world, no bustling self-importance."

I looked around, noticing a crowd of saints, all dressed the same as she. "Join us," they urged.

Sadly, I murmured, "I can't. Pray for me."

Struggling with personal difficulties of any kind leaves its mark: labels lived with, opportunities closed off, relationships broken. In some cases it seems as though we can't lose anything more. Yet God asks us to do just that. We have to lose all that blocks us from being single of heart, until we live completely in freely chosen dependence, in a life of simple beauties. God calls us out of the "big cities" of our aspirations to the bridges that shelter people who have no home in this world. We thought surviving loss, failure, or illness was a feat. Struggling with our ego in the downward journey staked out by the Christ of the Beatitudes is a far more turbulent and demanding call. For those who follow it, there is a creative peace; radiance surrounds all they are and do.

## CONTEMPLATION

### *"Blessed are the pure in heart"* (Mt 5:8 NRSV)

I love the translation of this beatitude in the Message Bible: "You're blessed when you get your inside world—your mind and heart—put right..." (Mt 5:8 MSG). But there is also something foreboding about this translation. The process of getting our attitudes, preferences, desires "put right" will lead us inevitably through loss, darkness, confusion, messiness—for most of the time we are at least a little attracted to things that don't leave our hearts "right."

I remember that in the first ten years after my stroke, I felt torn apart by highs and lows, breaking down every three years. I distinctly remember, however, an inner awareness that along with the manic-depressive symptoms there was a mysterious struggle being fought in my heart between reaching for the stars and living with my feet on the ground—illusion and reality, pride and humility, and an anxiety over what I had lost. Medication, therapy, and alternative modalities of healing have reined in my mood swings, but God and I still tussle over my disordered desires.

In the spiritual life there are phases. In the beginning we work on ourselves, trying to take on the mind and heart of Christ.

Prayer and spiritual reading, the sacraments and reading the word of God, spiritual direction and community are sources of strength and challenge, channels of grace and transformation. Nourishing ourselves on the presence of God who manifests himself through these means, we actively work to change our behaviors and attitudes and values to more closely reflect the nature of God. The stormy dark clouds of evil are gradually dispelled by the radiance of the One who resides in the core of our being.

Through the living of the Beatitudes, however, God begins to work on us. They reveal to us the attitudes most in common with God's heart, attitudes which are painfully countercultural, beyond our ability. In the Beatitudes, Jesus praises those for whom we often would feel sorry, especially if we are the ones who are mourning, poor, or persecuted. These are the people whom Jesus says most closely resemble him. These are the people who have reached their highest human fulfillment. These are the people who are in possession of the greatest good, which others have not yet been able to attain.

In the world of the Beatitudes, God attracts us so powerfully that we turn our eyes entirely toward him (and away from everything else), consecrating ourselves entirely to the glory of God. When our gaze is transfixed on God's glory so that we enter into the mystery of our being, we need to hang a big DO NOT DISTURB sign on the doors of our heart. At this point, God takes over. In order to make our hearts pure and clean, God invites us into a long period of darkness, much like a caterpillar that spins a chrysalis and waits in the shadows of a dormant hope. God comes in with a big bulldozer and starts to work. On the exterior we will experience unexpected reversal: broken relationships, disappointments, failures, illness, and misunderstanding. It will feel like the rug is being ripped out from under us. Indeed, it is, for God wants us to reach our highest ecstasy: to long for him, to cling to him with our whole being, to have nothing to offer of ourselves, to be totally dependent on him for everything: to be poor in heart. Our hearts will break as masks and illusions and scaffolding tumble to the ground, but in this poverty we will discover blessed freedom.

Even in the midst of ruinous circumstances, there will be an interior tug of war between cynicism and hope. In the midst of tears, we will cry out alternately in anger and in the blessed realization that something is emerging within us that is not of our making. God has drawn close to us and entered our solitude to share it with us, to stand in solidarity beside us in our mourning as the crucified and resurrected Lord, promising us life.

Gently we will allow a timid "new creation" to be coaxed from our hearts. Letting go of our past dreams, preferences, and expectations, we will take on much smaller goals. Instead of competing for the first place and the top position, we will discover that love is the most rewarding place of all. We will become free from all that ties us down because we realize we are always and everywhere loved by God. Because we have found our place in God's heart, we no longer need a place in the spotlight. As meek persons we will build up and recreate situations. As merciful people we become an extension of God's merciful love in the world.

We grow stronger as we refuse to be satisfied with anything less than God. Because the reign and primacy of God have become established in our soul, we refuse to accept injustice, violence, and war. We become people of justice, peacemakers who work so that the nature of God is reflected in creation, impatient with the impatience of God when people suffer at the hands of others' self-interest. We will work for the coming of the kingdom announced by Jesus Christ, extending the power of his message to others around us, with the weakness and vulnerability that marked his life.

From the darkness of waiting, the caterpillar emerges a beautiful butterfly. In the Beatitudes, Jesus says that the poor in spirit are blessed for "the kingdom of Heaven is theirs" (Mt 5:3 NJB). According to Erasmo Leiva-Merikakis, the people of the Beatitudes have become "members of the Kingdom that Jesus is."[3]

The emphatic sense of belonging puts the ones who live the Beatitudes "on a parity of status with the King himself.... By their radical poverty of existence, they have been made royal as Jesus is royal, since he is the King who stripped himself of all things except obedience to the Father's will."[4] As Jesus passes from death through the darkness of the tomb to resurrection, the one who lives the Beatitudes passes through the radical transformation of being raised from the experience of death and waiting, resurrected into a life of dependence.

What we once feared—no status, no address, no memory of "me," no place in the world, no bustling self-importance—we finally throw off as we run the race of life in the company of the saints.

## EXPLORING

- Have you received vital direction in your life during prayer? What was that advice? What changed because of it?

- In your experience has prayer been a source of guidance in the midst of difficulties? What has that been like?

- How would you respond to someone who said, "I wish God would just tell me what to do"? Do you think he does? How?

---

3. Erasmo Leiva-Merikakis, *Fire of Mercy, Heart of the Word: Meditations on the Gospel According to Saint Matthew,* vol. 1 (San Francisco, Ignatius Press, 1996), 187.

4. Ibid., 187.

•➤• Have you experienced within yourself the tug between dependence and interdependence with others, between importance and insignificance? What has that meant for your life? How have you or how could you find peace?

•➤• Are there aspects of your own interior world that you wish were "put right"? What are they? Have you brought this desire to prayer?

•➤• Has "anxiety over what you have lost" been an issue for you? How so?

•➤• Name some practices you have developed in the first phase of your spiritual development that have helped you grow in your relationship with God.

•➤• Have you experienced some signs that God is leading you on the path of the Beatitudes? What is that like?

•➤• Are you being drawn to countercultural values? What are they? What is this experience like? How do others react? What difficulties are you finding? What rewards?

•➤• How is God working right now in your life? Is it time to take your hands off your soul and give him free rein?

•➤• Does the image of the caterpillar and the butterfly speak to you? Are you going through a chrysalis stage of life? What is the waiting like? The darkness?

## LISTENING

Close your eyes and picture yourself on a pilgrimage. You could be going to a favorite place, a sacred silence, a city, the forest, or a desert. As you walk along, another pilgrim approaches you and promises that you will find the secret to a holier, happier life in that place. Let your imagination lead you into the place of your destination. What do you see? Whom do you encounter? What do you hear? What are you told? What are you feeling? What is your response?

## RESTING

Resting with these passages of Scripture can deepen your healing. To prepare yourself to rest deeply in your heart where healing can truly take place, you can repeat the listening prayer experience above before you use any of these Scripture passages, or you can place yourself into the scene described in the passage. Each time tell Jesus what you see and what you feel, and wait for him to say something to you.

### Crowd of Witnesses

Hebrews 11:13–40
Revelation 14:1–5

The Book of Hebrews has a wonderful hymn to the faith of those who have gone before us: the great people of faith such as Abraham, Sarah, Jacob, Moses, Rahab, David, and Samuel. These were people who kept their eyes focused on the future, on the city that God had waiting for them. They had their eyes on the One whom no one could see. They kept right on going through difficulties, walking toward the place of rest prepared for them by God. We know people perhaps among family or friends who fit into this group of pilgrims (cf. Heb 11:13–40). It isn't until the Book of Revelation that we get a glimpse of that city prepared for those who walk by faith and not by sight. We see thousands of people who have lived their lives on earth without compromise, dedicated to the Lord, the Lamb of God, and who now follow the Lord wherever he goes. These are the first fruits of the harvest of God. In this city there is an address for you, a place for you, a song only you can sing in honor of God. When you have to brave difficulties and mistreatment, keep your eyes on the One who loves you, though unseen, and on the crowd of people who have gone before you on the very same path and who now see what they once had longed for in faith (cf. Rev 14:1–5).

> All of these died in faith without having received the promises, but from a distance they saw and greeted them. They confessed that they were strangers and foreigners on the earth, for people who speak in this way make it clear that they are seeking a homeland. If they had been thinking of the land that they had left behind, they would have had opportunity to return. But as it is, they desire a better country, that is, a heavenly one. Therefore God is not ashamed to be called their God; indeed, he has prepared a city for them. (Heb 11:13–16 NRSV)

> Then I looked, and there was the Lamb, standing on Mount Zion! And with him were one hundred forty-four thousand who had his name and his Father's name written on their foreheads. And I heard a voice from heaven like the sound of many waters and like the sound of loud thunder; the voice I heard was like the sound of harpists playing on their harps, and they sing a new song before the throne and before the four living creatures and before the elders. (Rev 14:1–3 NRSV)

## What Counts Most in Life

Philippians 3:7–11
Psalm 51

One of my favorite passages from the Letters of Saint Paul is in his Letter to the Philippians. Paul lists a series of credentials that would have made him one of the up-and-coming Jewish leaders, obviously going places. He talks about his heritage, his

education, his religious attitudes and accomplishments, his virtue. On the road to Damascus, however, Paul had encountered
the risen Christ face-to-face, and all of this crumbled into dust.
He now considered them as "garbage"—not just second-rate, but
worthless enough to be discarded—compared with what mattered most: knowing Christ and gaining Christ. But this struggle,
no doubt, was a struggle Paul encountered again and again in his
life as his relationship with God deepened (cf. Phil 3:7–11).

King David, that wonderfully human figure whom God loved
so much, fought, as we all do, the inner battle of what counts
most in life. Transfixed by the beauty of another man's wife, he
decided to sleep with her, murdering her husband when she
informed him that she was pregnant. The marvelous stanzas of
Psalm 51 are traditionally understood as expressing David's sorrow as he realizes anew what counts in life.

> Yet whatever gains I had, these I have come to regard as loss
> because of Christ.... I regard everything as loss because of the
> surpassing value of knowing Christ Jesus my Lord. For his sake
> I have suffered the loss of all things, and I regard them as rub-
> bish, in order that I may gain Christ. (Phil 3:7–8 NRSV)

> Have mercy on me, O God,
> according to your steadfast love;
> according to your abundant mercy
> blot out my transgressions.
> Wash me thoroughly from my iniquity,
> and cleanse me from my sin. (Ps 51:1–4 NRSV)

## Inner Healing

Before beginning this section you may wish to pray with the
guided imagery contemplation found on page 9.

One of my favorite sayings comes from a simple cloistered nun who became a great saint: Thérèse of Lisieux. She said that the value of life depends not on the place we occupy, but on the manner in which we occupy that place. These words are a direct reflection of the first beatitude found in the Gospel of Matthew, "Blessed are the poor in spirit" (Mt 5:3 NRSV). In fact, all the Beatitudes are rooted in this call to be poor in spirit. Translated into modern contexts, this beatitude means that our life cannot be adequately measured by the accumulation of power, prestige, or possessions. Rather, our true worth comes from being beloved children of God who know how to respond in gratitude to God and how to serve our brothers and sisters. To be poor in spirit requires a continual inner assessment of thoughts, desires, and motivations—all the inner movements of our heart.

One of the best ways to keep watch over our hearts is to make some kind of consciousness examen every day. This examen can help us monitor the motives for our choices and actions. For instance, we could ask ourselves: Am I responding to life from the spirit of the Beatitudes or from the messages I pick up from advertisements and television? Is there a subtle attempt for a position of prestige underneath my volunteer project? Am I motivated by love for myself and others, or is there something else going on in my relationships? The examen can be a wonderful tool in our growth toward self-awareness.

The consciousness examen was initially formulated by Saint Ignatius in the sixteenth century as he shaped the spiritual exercises that are still helpful today for anyone who wants to grow in the spiritual life. Over the years, the way of doing the examen has been simplified for those who lead busy lives.[5] It can be as simple as taking some time every evening to ask two simple questions:

---

5. See Dennis Linn, Sheila Fabricant Linn, and Matthew Linn, *Sleeping with Bread: Holding What Gives You Life* (Mahwah: Paulist Press, 1994).

For what am I most grateful today?
For what moment am I least grateful today?
Or, When did I give and receive the most love today?
When did I give and receive the least love today?

When making the examen, I take time to express gratitude for the blessings received, and I look within myself to see what was going on during the time when I was least grateful. Was I trying to control? Was I jealous of what others received? Was I upset because I was not complimented on work done? Was I caught in a desire for power, possessions, prestige? The goal here is not to blame myself or others, but to gently surface what has been hidden from my eyes, even though it has been affecting my life and relationships. The most important part of the examen is to bring what I learn about my heart into the loving presence of Jesus. We cannot change anything within ourselves without this deep awareness.

Chapter Eight

# Meeting God in Unexpected Places

*"The Lord is about to pass by"*

 IMAGING

On a recent retreat I was struggling with the many hours that stretched through the week that were available for prayer and reflection. I was restless. I couldn't sit still for more than twenty minutes at a time. I felt I was going to waste this precious week of retreat. I was worried because I couldn't arrange and orchestrate and accomplish this retreat. For that moment I was unable to grasp the mystery that the best prayer is simply being attentive to God when he is passing by.

One morning I was sitting awkwardly in chapel for one of my "twenty minute marathons." I closed my eyes and pictured myself sitting next to Jesus. We were sitting along the bank of a beautiful lake, side by side. I was painfully aware of the weight of my defensiveness and anxiety, which I couldn't seem to shake. In my imagination Jesus stood up, dove into the lake, and swam across to the other side. I decided to follow. When I finally reached the other side and pulled myself up on the bank I was soaking wet and cold. Jesus covered me with a robe to keep me warm. When I looked at the garment he had given me, I realized it was exactly like his. I was dressed exactly like him. We sat together on the other side of the lake, a place of transformation to which he had brought me. I had not earned it, figured it out, learned about it. I had simply been brought there.

In the weeks that followed the retreat I began to learn what this place of transformation was all about. It certainly wasn't about perfection. That had been the trap of my lifetime. It was a place where I began to allow myself to experience my humanness, my tiredness, anger, desire, and self-righteousness—as frustrating and embarrassing as that was—so that I could begin to allow the "garment" of Jesus' thoughts and attitudes and desires to emerge, and the dross to wash away. Instead of trying to appear righteous or manufacture righteousness, I descended into the darkness of some very confusing internal dynamics. Staying with the anxiety, I eventually discovered that I am held there, that in the center of the mansion of my soul I am inhabited by the God who loves and upholds me. I do not need to achieve perfection. I only need to be in tune with my divine Master who transforms me into himself.

## CONTEMPLATION

*"The Lord is about to pass by" (1 Kings 19:11 NRSV)*

Elijah is a colorful and imposing Old Testament prophet who plods through the reign of Ahab, King of Israel, alternatively fearless and frightened, courageous and despondent. All in all, a very human guy, who knew how to wait on God's presence.

A core story of the Elijah cycle is his challenge to the 450 prophets of Baal. He calls the people of Israel together and says, "When are you going to decide who you will worship as God: the God of Israel or Baal? Make up your minds and follow the God who is the real God. Don't be hoodwinked by an imposter. And to help you out we'll have a contest. Come to Mount Carmel. Both the prophets of Baal and I will lay out a sacrifice to our respective gods. We will each call on our God. Whichever God answers by sending down fire to consume the sacrifice will prove himself to be the real God."

The people agree that this would answer the question for them once and for all. So they all gather on Mount Carmel. It is a fascinating passage that describes the events of that day (cf. 1 Kings 18:25–39). Elijah lets the prophets of Baal go first. They lay out the sacrifice and then pray to their god. "O Baal, hear us." Nothing. So they pray louder. Nothing. So they dance and jump and stamp on the altar. Nothing. Elijah taunts them, "Shout louder. Maybe he's sleeping!" Try as they might, the prophets can't force an answer from the heavens. No fire appears. Nothing. They demand that their god appear and perform for their sake. No god appears.

Then Elijah calls the people over to the altar he has built to the God of Israel. He prepares the sacrifice. He pours water on it till the sacrifice is soaked and the water is so abundant that it filled a moat around the altar. Then he prays. He doesn't yell. He doesn't dance. He doesn't jump or stamp. He simply says, "O God, make it known that you are God in Israel and I your servant. Reveal to this people that you are giving them another chance to repent." Immediately the fire of God falls on the altar and consumes the sacrifice. The people fall to the ground and worship God.

Elijah knew how God acted. He knew why God acted. And he knew God was faithful. He was attuned to what God desired. Elijah simply asked him to accomplish his desires. And all the people knew they were in the presence of God as they cried out, "You are the true God of Israel!"

Now this show of God's glory didn't win Elijah any friends with the political powers of the day. In fact, his life is now in danger. So he escapes to Beersheba, far in the south of Judah, and then travels alone into the desert. There he collapses, praying for death to end his troubles. An angel nudges him and tells him to get up and eat something since he had a long way to go. The mighty prophet from Mount Carmel is now powerless to sustain himself. The angel provides Elijah with a loaf of bread and some water. Nourished with this food, he walks all the way to Mount Horeb, forty days away. This is another name for Mount Sinai— the place where Moses encountered God face to face, where the Lord made a covenant with his people: he would be their God and they were to be his people.

There, on that sacred height, Elijah stands before the Lord, as long before Moses had done. And God passes by. Not in the powerful ripping of stormy wind, or devastating earthquake, or death-dealing fire. God is in the gentle and quiet whisper, more literally in "a sound of sheer silence" (1 Kings 19:12 NRSV), the only time this phrase occurs in the Old Testament. When Elijah hears the silence, he muffles his face in his great cloak. He knows he is in the presence of God.

Elijah had been to the heights of religious power and to the depths of despondency; he had been God's messenger and had had to wait on God's arrival on God's terms; he had been running from the law and had run into the arms of God. Elijah didn't live through these experiences woodenly. He thrilled in exaltation, he sank in despair, he raged, and he waited in silence; he feared for his life, and he gave up on life. We too live through experiences that force us to face complex psychodynamics. The way we have gone through life is called into question as we cross the desert, climb the mountain, or swim across the lake. Where once we thought we were right, we see we are wrong. More and more we realize in the second half of life that we have to take back everything we pontificated on in the first half of life. We discover the ugly motivations behind our good actions and our moral thrashing of others. We have to be willing to be clothed anew in the cloak of Jesus, to be fed by the angel in the desert, to be met by God in unexpected places and unfamiliar ways.

As God and we are more and more present to each other, we learn to become serene, to accept the flow of life, to acknowledge the healing power of the Love that lifts up the universe in its arms. We discover that life is okay in all its messiness, brokenness, and awkward transformations.

---

## Exploring

- How do you define prayer? Has your understanding of prayer shifted through the years? What was the catalyst for that change?

- Have you ever experienced prayer as "concentrated presence"? Do the words gazing, listening, learning, loving, hungering describe this experience of presence for you? Or would you use other words?

- Have you had an experience with God in which you felt a desire to give God everything? Has God asked everything of you? Can you talk about what this would mean for your life? What kind of feelings does it bring up in you?

⋅•⋅ Do you agree that "the best prayer is just being attentive to when God is passing by?" Can you talk about a "passing by" experience of the Lord in your life?

⋅•⋅ The image of Jesus swimming across the lake evokes transformation or transition. What other images have been transformative for you?

⋅•⋅ How has God asked you to change? What was that like? What gifts did you receive in that process?

⋅•⋅ If Jesus clothed you with a cloak similar to the one he was wearing, what would that cloak look like? What would it symbolize?

⋅•⋅ What is the difference between perfection and transformation? Why is transformation so difficult at times? Why does it create anxiety?

⋅•⋅ Do you stay quietly with uncomfortable feelings when they arise in order for them to settle and reveal their secrets to you? What would happen if you did? Do you have unhealthy ways of expressing or experiencing your feelings?

⋅•⋅ Saint Teresa of Avila, in her book *The Interior Castle*, speaks of God dwelling in the innermost room of our interior mansion. How would you picture this room? When you enter it what do you feel? What do you want to do? What is God's presence like?

⋅•⋅ Have you ever tried to make God perform like the prophets of Baal—to prove himself? What happened? What was different about Elijah's approach?

⋅•⋅ Describe your Mount Horeb experience—when God showed himself to you. Was it in power? Stillness? Beauty? Silence?

⋅•⋅ Do you agree that life in all its messiness is okay? Why or why not?

## LISTENING

In a quiet space, take some time to think about your life as it is right now. Make a list of events. As you list them, note your physical reactions to each of these events. Write these in a list. Draw a simple picture of yourself at this time of your life. List the feelings that arise in your heart. Now, in a quiet space, sit with Jesus on the side of a lake. Tell him how you are feeling. Watch his reaction. Is he facing you? What are his eyes saying? How does he show you he's listening? After a while he stands up. Follow him. He may swim across the lake. Perhaps he starts across a field or down a trail into the woods, or up a mountainside. Follow him to this new place in your life and in your relationship with him. When you arrive at the new place pay attention to what Jesus says or any symbols he uses to speak to you.

## RESTING

Resting with these passages of Scripture can deepen your healing. To prepare yourself to rest deeply in your heart where healing can truly take place, you can repeat the listening prayer experience above before you use any of these Scripture passages, or you can place yourself into the scene described in the passage. Each time tell Jesus what you see and what you feel, and wait for him to say something to you.

### The Abiding Presence

Exodus 24:9–18
Luke 1:26–38

When the chosen people who were fleeing from Egyptian slavery arrive at Mount Sinai, the Lord invites Moses and Aaron and the elders of Israel up the mountain. After they have seen God and have eaten and drunk in his company, Moses climbs up higher by himself to wait for God, who would write on tablets of stone the law and the commandments God was giving to his people. When Moses goes up the mountain, a cloud settles over Mount Sinai. The cloud covers the mountain and the Lord settles there. Later, when Moses has erected the tent of meeting according to the plan he was given on the mountain, the cloud again covers the sanctuary and the Lord's glory fills it. The Lord takes possession of his sanctuary. He promises to abide with his people in this holy space (cf. Ex 24:9–18). When the angel announces to Mary that she is to be the mother of God's Son, he tells her that in a mysterious way she will become like the Temple upon which the glory of the Lord rests: "You will be overshadowed by the Holy Spirit and your son will be the Son of God" (cf. Lk 1:26–38).

> Then Moses went up on the mountain, and the cloud covered the mountain. The glory of the LORD settled on Mount Sinai, and the cloud covered it for six days; on the seventh day he called to Moses out of the cloud. Now the appearance of the glory of the LORD was like a devouring fire on the top of the mountain in the sight of the people of Israel. (Ex 24:15–17 NRSV)

> The angel said to her, "The Holy Spirit will come upon you, and the power of the Most High will overshadow you; therefore the child to be born will be holy; he will be called Son of God." (Lk 1:35 NRSV)

## Deeply in Tune with the Father

Mark 15:25–39
Mark 16:1–20

On another mountain in Scripture people demand, "Show us God's power. Come down from that cross and we'll believe you are God's Son!" That mountain is Mount Calvary (cf. Mk 15:25–39). Jesus, however, is like Elijah—deeply in tune with the heart of his Father. Jesus doesn't demand the appearance of his Father to vindicate him in front of the people. He is committed to the plan devised by the Trinity for the salvation of the world. At the cost of his life, at the cost of proving himself in front of those who had demanded his death, he stays true to that plan. He trusts that the Father would be there for him and for all of us, even in the face of silence and absence, when he could no longer feel the Father's presence or his love (cf. Mk 16:1–20).

> It was nine o'clock in the morning when they crucified him. The inscription of the charge against him read, "The King of the Jews." And with him they crucified two bandits, one on his right and one on his left. Those who passed by derided him, shaking their heads and saying, "Aha! You who would destroy the temple and build it in three days, save yourself, and come down from the cross!" (Mk 15:25–30 NRSV)

> As they entered the tomb, they saw a young man, dressed in a white robe, sitting on the right side; and they were alarmed. But he said to them, "Do not be alarmed; you are looking for Jesus of Nazareth, who was crucified. He has been raised; he is not here. Look, there is the place they laid him. But go, tell his disciples and Peter that he is going ahead of you to Galilee; there you will see him, just as he told you." (Mk 16:5–7 NRSV)

## A Voice for Me

Mark 9:2–13
Luke 5:1–12

God speaks all through the Old Testament. He speaks to Adam and Eve in the Garden, to Cain and Abel, Abraham, Isaac, Jacob, Joseph, Moses, the prophets. He speaks with Jesus, and

Jesus speaks with people in the Gospels (cf. Mk 9:2–13). God turns up unexpectedly in the apostles' lives and addresses them directly (cf. Lk 5:1–12). He must also have a voice for me. By his very nature God communicates himself to us. He cannot be silent and withhold his life and love. He draws us into communion. Such intimacy between God and us demands a scriptural sense of time—ample, generous, free, whole. We can't show up and say to Jesus, "Okay. I can give you twenty minutes starting now," and then set an alarm to indicate the end of the conversation as if it were a wrestling match. This relationship, like any relationship, grows only when we give it time.

> Six days later, Jesus took with him Peter and James and John, and led them up a high mountain apart, by themselves. And he was transfigured before them, and his clothes became dazzling white, such as no one on earth could bleach them.... Then a cloud overshadowed them, and from the cloud there came a voice, "This is my Son, the Beloved; listen to him!" (Mk 9:2–3, 7 NRSV)

> Then Jesus said to Simon, "Do not be afraid; from now on you will be catching people." When they had brought their boats to shore, they left everything and followed him. (Lk 5:10–11 NRSV)

## INNER HEALING

Before beginning this section you may wish to pray with the guided imagery contemplation found on page 9.

God will be passing by.... Prayer is above all an attempt to be present to the God who is with me now. The more mindful I am of the present moment, the more I recognize that I am safe and secure in God's presence, consequently, the more I will be able to accept myself as I am and truly be who I most deeply am. I can stop trying to defend the masks that my ego wears.

When we are depressed, tired, anxious, overworked, or simply out of sorts, we tend to look at everything through dark glasses. This way of seeing sends us spiraling into a deep abyss. Hope and transformation seem completely out of our reach.

One of the best ways to change our way of seeing and being is to develop an attitude of gratitude. I remember clearly the day I came across the wise advice of the fourteenth-century Dominican mystic Meister Eckhart, that in our whole life only one prayer is absolutely essential: thank you. I had been feeling stuck, unable to pray, and hopeless about ever changing myself. I thought, this prayer was something I could do. It is something we all can do.

Stop several times during the day and simply be present to the moment. God is here. Can I be thankful? What has happened in the past few hours for which I am thankful? Can I begin to see the blessings that surround me?

Begin a gratitude journal in which you record every evening at least five things for which you are grateful. While this may seem to be a simple practice, it can reap tremendous benefits. It changes our way of seeing, and when God next passes by we will be ready to recognize God's presence in our lives and be more at peace with who he created us to be.

Chapter Nine

# The Secret of Beauty, Love, and Security

## *"You're beautiful with God's beauty"*

 IMAGING

Hope unfolds in our life when we are able to bring our history, our experiences, our feelings into our intimacy with the Lord. We can too easily fall into the trap of compartmentalization—keeping our relationship with God and our spiritual growth separate from a fight with our spouse, frustrations at work, or the pain we might still carry from an abusive childhood. God doesn't appreciate being kept in a box. He is yearning to involve himself in the "stuff" of our suffering, or, to use another metaphor, many times God and our lives are on two separate islands. How do we build a bridge on which Jesus can run across to embrace us and over which we can carry our weary hearts to give them to the Lord?

One day I was letting my mind roam through the changes in my attitudes and behavior over the past several years. A colleague had noted how controlling I had become as I struggled to create order out of a chaotic situation. Even though I knew she was right, I had tucked the comment away because I didn't understand the dynamics that were leading to this change in my leadership style. It was too difficult to acknowledge this negative turn in myself.

As I asked Jesus to help me understand what had been happening within me, a childhood memory popped into my mind. I was twelve years old and at home with my sister and brother while my parents ran an errand. We thought there was a bat downstairs, and my little brother decided he would go down and take care of it. As the one "in charge," I told him he couldn't, and a full scale argument ensued. As I thought of the story, I remembered the feelings of terror: how threatened I felt by the clearly exaggerated sense of doom created by what turned out to be a little bird, the fear of getting in trouble if something happened, the chaotic feeling of things getting out of control if my brother didn't do what I said.

This small baby-sitting event was a microcosm of the "catastrophizing" that often marks my approach to situations. By exploring it I could see the emotional programming underlying my recent turn in behavior. The experience also crystallized in a story some larger emotional filters that were skewing reality in an even more pervasive way in my life.

## CONTEMPLATION

*"You're beautiful with God's beauty" (Lk 1:28 MSG)*

Mary was also a young girl when something overwhelming happened to her. Instead of a bat in the house, an angel showed up in her room one day. Trying to look beyond the familiar, stilted holy-card renditions of the Annunciation, I imagine an angel walking up to a young teenage girl, holding her hands, looking into her eyes with great joy, and saying softly, "Mary, good day. I have special news for you. You are so beautiful, so full of grace, and God has sent me to tell you something very wonderful."

The Scriptures say Mary was frightened. That's probably an understatement. The simple world she had known had just been shaken by something quite extraordinary. When angels had appeared to her Jewish ancestors it meant God was intervening in a momentous, history-changing way. Mary was only a young teenager. Of course she wondered what this greeting could mean.

Her next move was very human: she tried to figure out the meaning of the angel's words. The angel, however, stopped her immediately and told her not to be afraid. God was going to be doing something. God had a surprise. She would be the mother of the Son of God who would rule the kingdom of David forever. Perhaps the first thing that ran through her mind was Joseph, to whom she was betrothed. Mary made an interjection, this time trying to figure out what she needed to do, since God's plans and her previous plans for her life didn't seem to be jibing. Again the angel reassured her. "God will do it. The power of the Most High will overshadow you, and your child will be the Son of God."

I love her response as given in the *Message Bible*: "Yes, I see it all now: I'm the Lord's maid, ready to serve" (Lk 1:37 MSG). In other words, "I get it. God's in charge here. I just need to do my duty."

And so Mary continued to be the simple woman of faith and endless trust in God through the birth of Jesus in a stable to his death on the cross; from the temple where Simeon told her that her heart would be pierced with sorrow to the public conversation when Jesus told his disciples that they were his mother, his brothers, his sisters now; from the miracle at the wedding in Cana to the first glimpse she had of him after the resurrection.

As the angel had told her, she was beautiful inside and out-side—full of grace. She was safe. She need not fear. This absolute certainty of being loved, wanted, and protected allowed her to remain simply herself during the glories and pain of the rest of her life.

Unlike Mary, most of us have a deep fear that we're unlov-able, not good enough, and that we will be thrown away if any-one finds out. It is this fear that causes us to develop a defensive lifestyle to protect ourselves. We develop habits of asserting con-trol, telling others what to do, overworking to ensure success, shining to attract attention, flirting to secure love. These habits go into effect whenever we feel threatened or overwhelmed, even when we can see they are not in our best interest.

We can pray ourselves into the events of the Scriptures in such a way that we allow God to heal our anxieties and relax our defensiveness. Closing my eyes I pictured the angel Gabriel com-ing to me in the midst of my argument with my brother. I let myself feel the anger I had felt that day when he pushed past me to go downstairs. As the rage started to recede I began to feel anxiety underneath. I had to keep things outside of me under control in order to keep control over my inner world. "Do it my way. No chaos!" I sat with the anxiety until it also burned away. Then I realized how I had built up the possibility of a bat in the basement into a huge monster that threatened our very lives. The sense of impending doom washed over me, and I could hardly breathe. I became overwhelmed with the responsibility of protecting others from certain death. Like a child, physically shaking, I hung on to the angel. Gradually I could hear his voice. "Kathryn, I have the same message for you that I had for Mary.

You are beautiful, filled with grace. God loves you. You are safe." I prayed with these words for many days. God makes me beautiful and loveable and protects me. I don't need to fabricate a simulation of beauty, love, or safety through control, power, or success because I can see myself through his eyes.

In time I could see that, like Mary, I could go through life without always fending off failure, criticism, or ordinariness. Like hers, my life would contain disappointment, chaos, and pain, and I would not be destroyed. I didn't have to be afraid that these would destroy me, because I had learned from her the secret of beauty, love, and security.

## EXPLORING

- How do you bring your life, your feelings, the movements of your heart into your prayer? Do you ask God for help? Do you search for meaning? Do you talk to God about your experience and ask him for guidance? What is unique to you and your relating with God?

- Do you feel any compartmentalization between God and your everyday life experience? Between what you see as good and bad in yourself, acceptable or unacceptable? Between your head and your heart, your thoughts and feelings? What would happen if there was more integration in your life?

- Have you ever asked Jesus to help you understand what was happening in your life or your feelings? What happened when you did? If you haven't, what is holding you back?

- Has someone made an observation to you recently about your attitude or behavior? What is your method of processing this type of feedback?

- Have you discovered a link between your adult attitudes, reactions, and behavior and a specific incident of your childhood? What keys to transformation did it give you?

- Close your eyes and hear God say to you, "You are beautiful. I love you. You are safe." What is your "feeling" response to this message?

- How do you seek to prove your beauty and goodness? In what way do you try to earn or attract love? What do you do when you feel insecure and anxious? How would your life change if you were convinced you were safely held in God's hands and were able to drop these behaviors?

## LISTENING

Using any of the Scripture passages below, bring something of your life into your intimacy with the Lord. Below is a suggested method that you may adapt to your needs. You will need a journal or paper and a Bible.

In your journal, briefly write out the event you want to bring to the Lord in prayer. As you are writing, pay attention to your physical reactions. Make a list of these: head pounding, stomach tight, difficulty breathing, and so forth. Then using simple stick-figure art, draw yourself in the situation the way you feel. You can add words to the picture if it helps you to access how the situation makes you feel. Make an exhaustive list of these feelings: angry, anxious, lonely, scared, uncertain, etc. Identify a time when you felt this way as a child. Take your time to let the memory surface. Draw yourself in the memory. Then read a passage from Scripture that helps you bring these feelings to Jesus (see suggested possibilities on next page). Become an active participant in the story, parable, or event. You can be someone in the Scripture passage itself, or a bystander from that time period, or you can be yourself as an adult or child interacting with Jesus in the context of the Scripture passage. Let the story unfold, taking its own path. Jesus will give you direction and guidance. As you pray, notice your affective movements. Sifting through these feelings will give you many insights into your personality and the process by which the Gospel questions, mends, and adjusts our spirit.

| | |
|---|---|
| Zacchaeus Climbs a Tree | Luke 19:1–10 |
| Who's in First Place? | Mark 9:33–37 |
| The Woman Anoints Jesus' Feet | Luke 7:36–50 |
| Jesus Walking on the Sea | Matthew 14:22–36 |
| Jesus in the Garden | John 20:1–18 |
| The Tax Collector and the Pharisee | Luke 18:9–14 |
| Paul Encounters Jesus | Acts 9:1–19 |
| The Transfiguration | Mark 9:1–8 |
| Jesus Washes the Disciples' Feet | John 13:1–17 |
| The Testing in the Desert | Matthew 4:1–11 |
| Story of the Lost Sheep | Luke 15:1–7 |
| The Prodigal Son | Luke 15:11–32 |
| Letting Out the Nets | Luke 5:1–11 |

## INNER HEALING

Before beginning this section you may wish to pray with the guided imagery contemplation found on page 9.

In her book *Hinds' Feet on High Places*, Hannah Hurnard tells the story of a young woman named Much-Afraid who escapes from her Fearing relatives in order to follow the Good Shepherd. Her journey is an interesting yet difficult one in which she faces things about herself that are hiding her true identity and hindering her ability to climb the High Mountain. Ultimately, she faces the truth about herself, and she is given a new name. She is no longer Much-Afraid. She is now called Grace and Glory.

This story is an allegory of the journey we must each make if we are to become whole and holy. In our youth and adolescence we are like sponges that easily absorb what people tell us. Too often we accept as true hurtful names that people call us and situations that happen for which we blame ourselves. Our adult years are spent discovering what these "untruths" are and shedding them. At the same time, we must claim the truth of how gloriously, wonderfully made we are!

Take time to make a list of the names you have been called in the past. Four-eyes, fat, string bean, ugly, stupid, or reject. The list could go on and on. Then, add the names that you have called yourself. Hopeless, awkward, big baby, chicken.... This list might also be quite long. Which of these names have you taken on as part of your identity? How often do you make choices or respond to people from a place deep within yourself that is wounded by hurtful names?

Take some time to pray. Imagine yourself sitting with Jesus. Can you ask him what is God's name for you? Is it Loved by God, Precious One, Chosen One, My Delight, Shining Star? Take the time to draw a shield or mandala or make a bookmark with your new name. Put this in a place where you can be reminded often of who you really are in God, in this place where you are always whole and united and loved.

Now take time to think of the significant people in your life. What names do you have for them? Can you think of a name that best reflects who these people are for you? You can help heal wounds and foster peace by reflecting to others the beauty of who they are. Why not make a drawing of the new name for each one of them?

Chapter Ten

# Realizing Who I Am

*"Your life repeated in my life"*

## Imaging

Healing is all about emerging from tight spaces into wide open places, moving from death to life, and transforming dullness into passion. We think we are living in freedom with passion, and we are, inasmuch as we are able. One day Jesus invites us closer, and we discover how confined and callous we've been. It's somewhat similar to love. A man and woman believe themselves to be loving people until they fall in love. Then they are overwhelmed with love's intensity and passion. After marriage they have to begin daily to choose to stay in love. And so it goes. Healthy people keep growing, and this transformation includes the pain of leaving behind and the awkwardness of moving toward the unknown.

An image came to me one day as I reflected on recent changes in my life. I felt as though I had been living in a cold, dirty, windowless room. I seemed so far from what Jesus was calling me to be. Difficulties had led me to feel like a failure. I knew, however, that this room was not all there was. This place, once my home, was now too small, too cold, too musty. I wanted out. I knew there was something beautiful on the other side of the walls.

I took an ax and began to hack at the walls. Little by little I tore down the thick wooden beams that surrounded me. As the first wall fell, a gust of fresh air came into the room, and I breathed as if for the first time. The scent of flowers made my heart skip a beat. The excitement gave me strength as I pulled down the entire structure that had confined me. I tossed a match onto the pile of wood and set it ablaze. Then I turned around.

A wide open field of flowers greeted my eyes. Butterflies, the traditional symbol of transformation, were flitting everywhere. I reached down and picked some flowers, making sure I stayed actively present in the image (not simply an observer).

"Here I am," I said to Jesus, and waited for him to come for me. After a while, I saw him walking toward me. He reached for my hands and folded me in an embrace. This is what God, religion, and spirituality are all about: the embrace of the divine Lover. Salvation history is the saga of the Father who wants to lavish his love, to empty himself in complete vulnerability that we, his creatures, might be the object of a love so selfless, so intense, and so complete that nothing is held back by this divine Lover.

Within me I felt the stirrings of love, or rather falling in love. Again Jesus covered me with his cloak.

## CONTEMPLATION

*"Your life repeated in my life" (2 Kings 2:9 MSG)*

One of my favorite passages of Scripture is the story of the prophet Elijah and his disciple Elisha immediately before Elijah left this earth.

Aware that he will soon be taken by God, Elijah begins a journey in three stages that progressively separates him from his people and his land. In a sense he is moving beyond the constriction of his prophetic history toward ultimate transformation. From the place called Bethel, Elijah travels with his disciple to Jericho, arriving at length at the Jordan River. There they cross the river into another land. The crossing of rivers is a profound biblical symbol: the crossing of the Red Sea was the demarcation that separated the Israelites from slavery as they entered freedom; the crossing of the Jordan was the point at which the people left their wilderness wanderings and entered the land promised them by the Lord. Moses, however, did not cross the river with them. He died on Mount Nebo after being given a vision of the land his people would possess. Now Elijah is crossing the Jordan, leaving the Promised Land, separating himself from his people, preparing to leave this earth.

Elijah asks Elisha if there is anything he can do for him before he is taken away. Without blinking an eye, Elisha responds: "Please, let me inherit a double portion of your spirit" (2 Kings 2:9 NRSV). A paraphrase of this response that has meant a lot to me is: "[I want] your life repeated in my life. I want to be a holy man just like you" (2 Kings 2:9 MSG).

I imagine Elijah scratching his head as he mumbles, "That's quite a big request. I'm not sure if I can actually obtain that for you. But, nevertheless, if you see me taken from you, you know your desire is granted."

Elisha stays close to Elijah as they walk. He is watching as fiery horses and a chariot come and whisk Elijah off in a whirlwind to heaven. Elisha calls after his beloved Elijah, but there is no response. The great prophet is gone. The dust settles around him as Elisha realizes that he is now alone. Now he is left to carry on the prophetic task in the land of Israel. In sadness, Elisha takes off his robe and tears his garment in two. Reaching down, he picks up Elijah's cloak, carries it back to the Jordan, and strikes the water with Elijah's cloak. The river divides and Elisha walks through, back to the Promised Land.

In his letter to the Christians at Colossae, Saint Paul continues this biblical image of a change of garments. In the paraphrase from the *Message Bible*, his meaning strikes home. Paul says, "You're done with that old life: It's like a filthy set of ill-fitting clothes you've stripped off and put in the fire. Now you're dressed in a new wardrobe. Every item of your new way of life is custom-made by the Creator, with his label on it. All the old fashions are now obsolete.... So, chosen by God for this new way of love, dress in the wardrobe God picked out for you: compassion, kindness, humility, quiet strength, discipline. Be even-tempered, content with second place, quick to forgive an offense. Forgive as quickly and completely as the Master forgave you. And regardless of what else you put on, wear love. It's your basic, all-purpose garment. Never be without it" (Col 3:9–10, 12–14 MSG).

In a gesture that reaches deep into this biblical symbolism, we can imaginatively tear into pieces mental "photos" of our past life, images that represent ways of living, reacting, behaving, thinking, and desiring that no longer fit. The Spirit invites us to pick up the cloak Jesus has left behind for us. What is this new garment like? What do we feel like when we wear it? How will it affect the way we think, desire, love, and behave? These are important questions as we grow into this new wardrobe, a process that takes a lifetime. Along the way we discover new "fashions," colors, sizes, and styles. Exchanges and trade-ins allow us to accumulate more and more of the Lord's wardrobe as we outgrow some of the garments we've worn.

We all experience what Saint Paul felt when he observed: "I do not understand my own actions. For I do not do what I want, but

I do the very thing I hate" (Rom 7:15 NRSV). Dynamics of personality, issues from our past, situational realities, and health factors are among many things that can contribute to conflicted feelings, compulsive behavior, and confused decisions. A poor spiritual self-awareness and a cooled relationship with God can be the result of these other factors in our life when they are unaddressed. We pray. We read the Bible. We resolve to change, but something stronger than us and our spiritual resolve keeps us from putting on the garments of the Spirit in any consistent way.

I run into this problem whenever I want to do something for my own physical or emotional well-being. I have decided time and again, for example, that I want to start walking daily. For the sake of my health I know I should start walking. Actually I would enjoy the time alone that I would have if I would just start walking. In the end, however, I never start walking. Why?

I didn't realize there were powerful dynamics going on within me that prevented me from taking up this activity that would be physically and emotionally beneficial to me. One of the strongest fears I have is the fear of failure. Deep down there is this hidden fear of deficiency, and work at times can become a way of hiding this pain from myself. As silly as it seems, a part of me thinks that if I stop working the world will crumble and my survival will be in jeopardy. Work hides my inner sense that I have not stayed connected to my deepest core. Putting in front of myself an image of a healthy person is not going to be enough to get me out walking. Nor is an image of a slim person. I already hate myself enough without getting into the whole dieting scene. Only after I look gently at why I feel I am a failure and where that fear of unworthiness comes from, only after opening myself to feel the fear (instead of running from it), will I discover that everything—success and failure—is part of divine Providence, all woven into the mystery of the glory of God. Once I embrace reality as it is instead of trying to make it different, I can let things be. I don't need to change them by working and controlling. Joy and gratitude well up in my heart.

Deep down I am a person who loves quiet, private time, solitude, nature, depth. Living in overdrive is not me. That is the "me" conditioned by life's circumstances, and thus I live in this defensive condition. But in reality, everything is already secure because God has made it so. Paul would say: "Seeing that while we were living as his enemies God sent us Jesus Christ to save us, won't he give us everything else we need besides? We are now in the Spirit who has made us the sons and daughters of God!" (cf. Rom 5:10). Taking a walk then expresses the fulfillment welling up in my soul from the realization of what God has done for me and who I am. Realizing this, I can walk away from my desk and enjoy the fresh air and solitude a walk would bring.

## Exploring

- What are symbols of healing or transformation that have been meaningful or powerful in your life?

- Is there a call for you to emerge from a constricted place into a space of greater freedom? What are your feelings about that possibility? How can you imaginatively connect with this reality within you? How do you picture where you are now? How do you envision the future gift?

- Have you ever said to Jesus in prayer, "Here I am, Jesus. I am waiting for you?" What would happen if you did?

- Do you agree that religion and spirituality are about love? There is no wrong or right answer. At different times in our life aspects of God and spirituality stand out and call for changes in thinking, willing, behaving.

⌁ If Jesus said to you, "Before I go is there something you want me to do for you?" what would you ask for? After you decide, find a passage in the Gospel in which someone is asking Jesus for a similar thing.

⌁ Is the image of a change of garments meaningful to you? Why or why not?

⌁ Draw a picture of your old "wardrobe," the "ill-fitting clothes" that have become compulsions or fixations in your life. How do these make you feel? Then draw a picture of your new "wardrobe" provided by the Spirit. Make a complete inventory of your new clothes. As you read through this list, how do you feel? Identify certain situations in your life that trigger in you behavior that is frustrating or hurtful. See whether you can identify any elements of your old "wardrobe" that are part of the cycle of your response. Then take the situation, and your new "wardrobe," and make a new plan of action for those situations.

⌁ Talk (or write) about a situation in which you seem blocked from making the next best choice. What fears or desires might be at the root of this difficulty? Talk to God about what you discover.

⌁ Is the distinction between who you are and what you are doing helpful for you in understanding your spiritual work?

## LISTENING

Set aside time to reflect on the way God is working in your life. Ask the Holy Spirit to provide you a symbol of where you are and where you are being called. Take some time to explore the image of your present life, with its parameters, boundaries, fixations, constrictions. How does this image make you feel? Pay attention to your physical reaction as you investigate every corner of the image symbolizing your present reality. List the thoughts and feelings that run through your mind and heart. Draw a picture of where you are. Jesus comes to you and offers you a way out to a larger, more beautiful space. He may give you an ax to cut down the walls, or a staircase to climb out, or he may lift you out. Leave the past behind and spend some time in the image of the call you are being given. What do you see? Hear? Feel? What do you desire? Tell Jesus, "Here I am. I am waiting for you." Wait for him to come. What does he say to you?

## RESTING

Resting with these passages of Scripture can deepen your healing. To prepare yourself to rest deeply in your heart where healing can truly take place, you can repeat the listening prayer experience above before you use any of these Scripture passages, or you can place yourself into the scene described in the passage. Each time, tell Jesus what you see and what you feel, and wait for him to say something to you.

### Rising from the Dead

> John 11:17–44
> Luke 24:1–6

All four Gospels tell the story of Jesus being placed in the tomb, but there are two "tomb" stories in the Gospel of John. Lazarus, Jesus' friend, falls ill and dies. He has been buried four days before the Lord appears. Later Jesus himself has died and is buried three days. The darkness of the tombs, the finality of death symbolized by the stone covering the mouth of the caves in which they have been buried, the burial cloths—each of these elements accentuates the distance between this life and death (cf. Jn 11:17–44). Sometimes we feel this "death" also. Because of sin, disillusionment, failure, depression, painful situations, illness, or grief over another's sorrow, we may feel as though we have been laid in a tomb. We may feel trapped, hopeless, blind. What must it have been like for Lazarus to hear the voice of his friend Jesus calling his name, to see a shaft of light coming into the cave after the stone had been rolled away, to hear the nervous silence of the crowd, to test his fingers—can he wiggle them? His legs—can they hold his weight? To pull the bandage from his eyes . . . just to see the way. A possible direction for prayer is to imagine Jesus calling you out of whatever tomb you are in. He unwraps the garments that have held you bound. He offers you food. As in the resurrection of Jesus, imagine people looking for you in the tomb and meeting angels announcing that you are not there anymore. They need to look for you among the living (cf. Lk 24:1–6).

> And Jesus looked upward and said, "Father, I thank you for having heard me. I knew that you always hear me, but I have said this for the sake of the crowd standing here, so that they may believe that you sent me." When he had said this, he cried with a loud voice, "Lazarus, come out!" The dead man came out, his hands and feet bound with strips of cloth, and his face wrapped in a cloth. Jesus said to them, "Unbind him, and let him go." (Jn 11:41–44 NRSV)

> They found the stone rolled away from the tomb, but when they went in, they did not find the body. While they were perplexed about this, suddenly two men in dazzling clothes stood beside them. The women were terrified and bowed their faces to the ground, but the men said to them, "Why do you look for the living among the dead? He is not here, but has risen." (Lk 24:2–5 NRSV)

## New Directions

 Acts 2:1–4

 Colossians 3:1–4

When we break out of a tomb our eyes need to adjust to the light. Coming out of a spiritual place of darkness and inner death, however, is the work of God and is followed by his powerful visitation. After the apostles had betrayed and abandoned Jesus at his arrest, hidden in a secret room to save their own lives, and met with Jesus when he appeared among them after his resurrection, they waited again in Jerusalem, in the upper room, for the gift of the Spirit Jesus promised to send (cf. Acts 2:1–4). After the death of their dreams, illusions, selfish expectations, and false selves, they were ready now to grow, to live, to move, to proclaim what they had witnessed. The Spirit made that possible by breaking open their present and making possible a new future! (cf. Col 3:1–4)

> When the day of Pentecost had come, they were all together in one place. And suddenly from heaven there came a sound like the rush of a violent wind, and it filled the entire house where they were sitting. Divided tongues, as of fire, appeared among them, and a tongue rested on each of them. All of them were filled with the Holy Spirit and began to speak in other languages, as the Spirit gave them ability. (Acts 2:1–4 NRSV)

> So if you have been raised with Christ, seek the things that are above, where Christ is, seated at the right hand of God. Set your minds on things above. (Col 3:1–2 NRSV)

## It Is Not I Who Live

 Galatians 2:19–21

 Romans 12:3–21

Just as Elisha wanted to live with the spirit of Elijah, repeating his teacher's life in his own, Paul wanted to live the life of Christ so that anyone who saw him would see Christ. When Paul makes his "It is not I who live" statements he is saying several important things. First, although our culture prizes autonomy and the isolated existence of the person who is out for himself or herself, it would be preposterous for a Christian to live this way. For Paul it would be like an arm or a leg trying to have an independent existence. In reality they are parts of a larger whole. All the parts work together and feel together. A Christian's existence implies loving, without which a Christian is nothing. To love and be loved is the essence of Christianity. When Paul states that it is no longer I who live but Christ who lives in me, he is stating that the independent self that the world takes as normal is absorbed into the authenticity of Christian community (cf. Gal 2:19–21). We belong because we share a common existence. We are parts of a single body: the body of Christ. We are tied together through love. As arms and legs are differentiated in the body, they are identified by the service in their various capacities to the body. Each has a different spiritual gift necessary for the common good of the community. For a Christian, the authentic use of "I"—the first person singular—must always be a variation of "I exist to serve you." "I exist to love you." "I exist because I am loved by you." "I exist because I am loved like you." When deciding on a course of action, the Christian needs to ask: Will the decided course of action empower or destroy others? (cf. Rom 12:3–21)

> It is no longer I who live, but it is Christ who lives in me. And the life I now live in the flesh I live by faith in the Son of God, who loved me and gave himself for me. (Gal 2:20 NRSV)

> For as in one body we have many members, and not all the members have the same function, so we, who are many, are one body in Christ, and individually we are members one of another. We have gifts that differ according to the grace given to us: prophecy, in proportion to faith; ministry, in ministering;

the teacher, in teaching; the exhorter, in exhortation; the giver, in generosity; the leader, in diligence; the compassionate, in cheerfulness. Let love be genuine; hate what is evil, hold fast to what is good; love one another with mutual affection; outdo one another in showing honor. (Rom 12:4–10 NRSV)

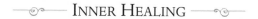

## INNER HEALING

Before beginning this section you may wish to pray with the guided imagery contemplation found on page 9.

There is a wonderful little story I heard long ago that comes from one of the Desert Abbas or Ammas. It tells of a young person who asked advice about prayer. Rather than answering the request for advice directly, the wise one responded with an example. The nature of water, he explained, is to be fluid and yielding, and the nature of the stone is to be hard. Yet, when water drips, drop by drop, over a long period of time, it will wear a hole in the stone. In the same way, the Word of God is gentle and tender, and the human heart can be hard as stone. But when people expose themselves over time to God's Word and God's Spirit, their hearts are softened and transformed.

When I first heard this piece of ancient wisdom I recognized that often I was merely "spinning my wheels" with all my attempts to change myself. I was working too hard and not leaving space for God. The desert wisdom of the ones who had gone before on this path invited me instead to consciously create time and space every day for God's Spirit to "drip" into my heart and transform me.

Soon after that, I found myself sitting in prayer holding a small bowl I had made in a pottery class. I quieted my mind and simply sat begging God to soften and transform my heart. The piece of pottery became my begging bowl. Shortly after this experience, I learned that the Japanese word for begging bowl is oryoki, which literally means "just enough." This became a way for me to intentionally beg for God's help. It is a contemplative and simple prayer anyone can practice.

I would encourage you to consider your prayer time as your begging bowl. Perhaps sit with your hands cupped in the form of a bowl. Take a few deep breaths, remembering that God is as close as the air you breathe. Clear your mind. Hand over any concerns you might have at this moment to God. Sit quietly, begging God to "drip" into your heart and to fill you with just enough for today.

When you are finished, offer a prayer of gratitude.

We do not transform ourselves. God transforms us. Our task is to be ready and open to receive what God desires to give us.

Appendix One

# Everyday Practical Choices for Healing and Hope

Over the past few years, a television program called *Extreme Makeover* has been very popular. In it a deserving family has their home demolished and, with the help of volunteers, a brand new home built in the very same spot. I've often thought how wonderful it would be if I could be totally transformed in the same way. I would want to be rebuilt whole, healthy, and holy.

However, we all know that people are much more complex than houses, and it isn't so easy. Besides, our broken places are actually some of our greatest blessings if we can discover the precious treasure they hold. So, how can you stay the course from healing to hope? Make small choices that enable you to change and grow. That's all. Everyday small, continuous decisions, one after the other, like placing one foot in front of the other.

## Step 1: Balance

Make a commitment to maintaining balance in your life. Balance work with play; activity with reflection; watching TV with reading a book; surfing the Internet with silence; companionship with solitude. We need to do this because expectations, needs, desires, and personal fragility, as well as other persons, pull us strongly in many directions at once. This will be easier if you have someone with whom you can speak about your life and to whom you can be accountable: a friend, a therapist, a spiritual director, or a life coach.

## Step 2: Make Concrete Lists

Create a list of what you know fosters spirituality, physical well-being, and emotional health in your life. Your list may differ somewhat from the lists of others because you are a unique person with particular God-given gifts and calls. Be sure that each of the items on the list is concrete and measurable and that each item can realistically be accomplished on a regular basis. Be careful because one of the great pitfalls is setting standards so high that you are bound to fail.

## Step 3: Draw Up a Spiritual Plan

What helps you nurture your spirituality? Is it reading? Listening to music? Taking a walk in nature? Praying the rosary? Everyone is different. God speaks to each of us in different ways and in a variety of times and places. For a while observe yourself; see where you feel God's presence most deeply. In what spiritual activity? Determine what is most helpful for you and draw up a small spiritual plan that will help you grow as a God-filled person. Be detailed! What practices will you build into your life? How often will you do them? Every day? Three times a week? Once a week? Where will you do them? What will you need to change in your schedule to make time for these spiritually nurturing activities? What do you hope to achieve by accomplishing them? Write out a vision of who you hope to be in six months time if you are faithful to this spiritual plan. What do you see changed? Improved? Eliminated from your life? How will it affect your relationship with others? Your relationship with God? How you feel about yourself? You decide on the extent of your plan, but be sure that it is realistic for you.

## Step 4: Lay Out a Program for Health

Follow the same process as above to determine what you need to incorporate in your life to improve or maintain your physical health. Do you need to walk more? Do you need to get more or less sleep? Do you need to eat more balanced meals? Do you need more or less exercise? Do you want to try acupuncture or nutritional counseling? Again, be specific. If you are going to walk to get more exercise, then determine when you'll walk, with whom, for how long, where, and what you will do during inclement weather or long winter months (depending on where you live). You may want to talk to your doctor before beginning a strenuous exercise program or alternative health modality.

## Step 5: Attend to Emotional Well-being

After reflecting and making a plan to attend to your spiritual and physical health, take adequate care for your emotional well-being. In today's hurried and harried society this part of your program for continued healing is crucial. The differences that exist between the emotional lives of one person and another are pronounced. I can only list some possibilities here to get you started. You may want to share your choices with a spiritual director, counselor, or friend, or bring them to a group that focuses on emotional health. Do you need more silence in your life or less? Do you need more solitude, or do you need to connect with others? Are you aware of your feelings, or is the expression of your emotions disrupting your life? Do you have someone with whom you can share what you are feeling? Do you keep a journal or paint? Have you lived through recent stress-filled situations such as a job loss, the death of a loved one or friend, an increased workload, the birth of a child, retirement, or divorce? How is this situation affecting you? Have you taken sufficient time to process what you have experienced? What will make you feel more whole and less fragmented, deeper and less shallow, more in control and less chaotic?

## Step 6: Start Small and Keep Going

Decide on one or two items from each category above and talk with someone about the commitment you are making to a healthier lifestyle. Keep account of how faithful you are to your choices. If you fail, perhaps you need to adjust what you are doing. Be gentle with yourself at all times, and try to network with others who have the same goals for a more hope-filled life.

Holding on to hope can be difficult when everything around us seems to be crumbling. We need to do our part in maintaining a lifestyle that will foster health, well-being, and holiness. But ultimately we cannot do this alone. We need to be open to God's grace, and we need the support of others. As we continue the journey to wholeness, let us not forget that God never asks the impossible. We are called to set out in faith, one step at a time, with the sure knowledge that we are loved unconditionally by the God whose name is Love.

Appendix Two

# A Process for Putting On Christ in Seven Stages

Saint Paul shows us in his life and in his letters that Christ is intent on saving us. He invites us to "put on Christ." In his letters, we can trace a process for this transformation that is deeply human and profoundly divine.

## Stage 1: *Reflect on unexpected encounters with God in your life.*

Paul tells the story of his meeting Christ on the road to Damascus three times in the Acts of the Apostles (cf. Acts 9, 22, 26). He obviously had reflected on the event, what it had meant, and how it had defined his life. When he had to describe who he was and explain what he was about, he recounted again the story of his encounter with the Lord on the road to Damascus. What happened in that encounter with the Lord? A Pharisee, zealous for the Law, intent on protecting Judaism from the ideas of these followers of Jesus, came face-to-face with the One he was fighting against. He discovered he had been wrong. Jesus, whom the followers of the Way claimed was alive, really was alive. Paul had seen him. Or rather he had been seen by him. In that encounter he realized his life mattered to God beyond his wildest dreams. God cared enough about Paul to save him from his misguided zeal. Paul's greatest dreams for himself perhaps included authority and prestige. God, however, had much bigger plans for Paul. He had plans that encompassed the whole world and the rest of history until the end of time. Paul didn't ask to get out of his calling like some of the great prophets in the Old Testament; Moses and Jeremiah, to mention two. He did exactly what he was told, and his little future of self-importance burst into a life of praise and glory.

It was clear to Paul that salvation and healing come from outside. We are reached out to by a divine Lover who wishes to draw our lives into his desires for the world. "For I want you to know, brothers and sisters, that the Gospel that was proclaimed by me is not of human origin; for I did not receive it from a human source, nor was I taught it, but I received it through a revelation of Jesus Christ....When God, who had set me apart before I was born and called me through his grace, was pleased to reveal his Son to me, so that I might proclaim him among the Gentiles" (Gal 1:11–12, 15–16 NRSV).

This one-on-one encounter with a God who wants to take over our life is possible also for us—perhaps this meeting between you and the divine Lover has already happened. Maybe we have met him and forgotten, returning to our old, small visions of who we are and what we can do. Paul invites us to a kenotic dynamic—a process of transition from who we are now to who God wants us to be.

## Stage 2: Make a distinction between who you are and what you are doing.

Paul introduces his letters consistently with phrases such as: "Paul and Timothy, servants of Christ Jesus, to all the saints in Christ Jesus who are in Philippi" (Phil 1:1 NRSV); "Paul an apostle ... to the churches of Galatia" (Gal 1:1, 2 NRSV); "Paul, called to be an apostle of Christ Jesus by the will of God ... to the Church of God that is in Corinth" (1 Cor 1:1, 2 NRSV). He never states what he was doing (writing a letter to a specific Church) without also stating who he is. First he is an apostle in relationship with Christ Jesus. Second he is sent to a particular community to announce Christ to the Gentiles. This enables Paul to go over and over again what it means to be an apostle of Christ Jesus. What are the characteristics of apostleship? What were the characteristics of Jesus' life? What has he been taught by Jesus throughout his life? This gives Paul a list of core qualities that help him know who he is made to be in his deepest core: another Christ, a servant and ambassador of reconciliation, someone who lives no longer for himself but for the glory of God.

Secondly, he is sent to the Corinthians, the Philippians, the Romans, the Galatians. His relationship with each of these groups of people is conflicted, tumultuous, and filled at times with disappointment. Paul reacts. He writes fiery letters; he sheds tears; he gets into arguments; he sends young disciples back home; he makes rash decisions. All of us in heated situations react. Our buttons get pushed, and we say and do things that are out of character. We each have our unique ways of dealing with pressure or fear or abandonment. A secret to spiritual growth is being able to distinguish the characteristics of our deepest core self from our defended or reactionary self.

*Stage 3: Put yourself squarely in the present and experience*
*what is happening without needing it to be different.*

Saint Paul embraced the present no matter what it brought. Shipwreck or fighting for the faith of his communities, preaching or stoning, hungering or feasting, he had learned to live it all without avoiding it, clinging to it, overreacting to it, needing it to be something else. Appreciate your inner and outer reality with serenity. Allow your experience to be what it is, without labeling it or fighting it. Only with serenity will we be able to understand our reactions.

The more we become centered within, get out from under the inner critic, and accept both the positive and negative parts of ourselves, the more our soul will relax.

Paul had many reasons to judge himself. He himself tells how he had rounded up followers of Jesus, locking them up in jail. In fact, the Acts of the Apostles makes clear that he stood in the crowd that stoned the deacon Stephen. The Acts of the Apostles states clearly that those who were stoning Stephen laid their cloaks "at the feet of a young man named Saul" (Acts 7:58 NRSV) and that "Saul approved of their killing him" (Acts 8:1 NRSV).

Paul's relationship with the Corinthians was stormy to say the least, partly due to the way he handled a thorny situation in the community. He had been sent to the Gentiles to announce the good news of salvation, a mission that was to ruffle the feathers of the nascent Christian community in which many were satisfied with retaining Jewish customs and restricting themselves to Jewish circles. Even the collection for the poor in Jerusalem, which he had so solicitously made for years, was, in the end, rejected. Paul could have spent a lot of time worrying about hurt feelings, relationships with authority, broken friendships, wondering what did I do wrong?

Instead, Paul lived through the roller coaster of his life and eventually reached the conclusion that we are all called for glory. "We know all things work together for good for those who love God, who are called according to his purpose. For those whom he foreknew he also predestined to be conformed to the image of his Son, in order that he might be the firstborn within a large family. And those whom he predestined he also called; and those whom he called he also justified; and those whom he justified he also glorified" (Rom 8:28–30 NRSV). Paul realized our inner completeness as sons and daughters of God created in the image of God and made resplendent with God's glorious grace freely bestowed on us in Christ (cf. Eph 1:6). When we reach the point where we know we are held by God's love in Christ Jesus, our heart opens, no longer held in the vice grip of fear.

## Stage 4: Acknowledge the deep drives within and let go of defensiveness.

When we begin to penetrate our inner drives we don't always like what we see. We discover the way we cover up our deepest fears, often projecting them outward onto others. Unable to face our own vulnerability, we see others as bad and flawed. A bit of conceit tinges the beauty of everything we do. By making ourselves out as better than the others we don't have to face our own failings. Paul, as Saul, had to acknowledge this in himself. He had a lot going for him before he met Christ. As a Pharisee, he was on an upward climb in religious circles. Suddenly, Jesus plunged him into blindness and completely turned the tables on him. Instead of persecuting the Christians, he needed to depend on them for salvation and life. For many years he must have worked on himself so that the new direction of his life would be manifest in every aspect of his thoughts, desires, preferences, and behavior. He wrote, "If anyone else has reason to be confident in the flesh, I have more: circumcised on the eighth day, a member of the people of Israel, of the tribe of Benjamin, a Hebrew born of Hebrews; as to the law, a Pharisee; as to zeal, a persecutor of the Church; as to righteousness under the law, blameless. Yet whatever gains I had, these I have to regard as loss because of Christ. More than that I regard everything as loss because of the surpassing value of knowing Christ Jesus my Lord" (Phil 3:4–8 NRSV).

Each of us can write a similar statement about what we have left behind to follow Christ. "I once was ... I once thought I was lucky because I.... I was secure because I collected.... I knew I was a great person because I used to.... But now I throw this all away. I realize it had no worth whatsoever. I want only Jesus, not my perfection or security or happiness. Knowing Jesus is more important to me than any of this. To share his sufferings is my greatest joy because I know he will let me share his resurrection." It is as if the toy box of our heart is revealed to be an empty, lonely place; after the entertainment stops and the others go home, we can begin to discover our soul.

## Stage 5: Acquire downward mobility. Live like God.

Central to Paul's thought is the mind-boggling, awesome story that God became man. That is—in case we haven't been duly impressed by this event—the Son of God left his place with his Father and his equality with God, and willingly became man, born of the Virgin Mary. He wasn't born in a palace appropriate for his importance. He was born where the animals were kept, with a bit of straw swept from the ground to keep him warm. Thus began thirty-three years in which the Son of God experienced and endured every aspect of our life, including temptation. He experienced hunger, thirst, exhaustion, frustration, dependence, misunderstanding, failure, the feeling of being trapped, and finally death itself. He didn't die in royal splendor, but as a criminal in the most ignominious death possible at the time (cf. Phil 2:6–8). Curiously, though, Christ Jesus became a human, willingly leaving his place as God and making himself a slave. It is the human tendency to want to climb to the top, to want—if it were possible—to become God. We want to be in control, to decide what is good, to be free of suffering. Jesus instead plotted out a very different way to be human, countering each of these three human needs. He submitted himself to the control of others; his fate was decided by others who determined what was right and good; and he willingly embraced suffering. The step we need to take, therefore, is to stop playing God and to embrace our humanness—the glory of our humanity as shown to us by Christ Jesus.

## Stage 6: Discover a heart set free.

At the deepest layer of transformation we find inner peace— clear, unclouded, and untroubled stillness. Our consciousness calms and is less ruffled by the events of life. Our heart opens, our mind relaxes, and our perception becomes more transparent. Saint Paul had much to say about the human heart because he had wrestled so much with his own. He knew its fear, its conceit, and its enormous capacity to love. You are all members of one body, he wrote to a community of Christians torn into factions by competition and pride. Love and service are the operative words. Just as a leg doesn't exist by itself, or an arm, or an ear, so you don't exist by yourselves. You exist only in service to the whole. When you embrace the downward direction of Christ's life, you don't discover defeat and death. You discover your heart and your capacity to live deeply and divinely. To the Corinthians, after instructing them that some are called to be apostles, others prophets, others teachers, others miracle workers, and so on, he urges an end to competing for roles, instead exhorting them to be ambitious for what means more than all these things: love (cf. 1 Cor 12:27–31).

Any of the roles we compete for or try to excel at without the exercise of love are of no use. "Though I command languages both human and angelic—if I speak without love, I am not more than a gong booming or a cymbal clashing. And though I have the power of prophecy, to penetrate all mysteries and knowledge, and though I have all the faith necessary to move mountains—if I am without love I am nothing" (1 Cor 13:1–2 NJB).

For Paul, what are the characteristics of love? What does love look like? He describes this love in his letter to the Corinthians. Many times we read Paul's characteristics of charity as if they were moral marching orders. Do this and you shall live! However, if we look more closely, we will see that he describes here a person emptied of all competition, fear, and self-righteousness. Such a person doesn't need to lash out or say cruel things because he is not afraid and not defending anything. She isn't conceited or boastful because she isn't competing to get anywhere or acquire anything. This heart isn't rocked with inner movements of resentment, spite, or anger because it is comfortable seeing others as better than itself. This freed heart delights in the truth because, rather than put a spin on things only to protect itself or get what it wants, it is ready to excuse, believe in the truth, hope, and endure whatever comes (cf. 1 Cor 4–8).

## Stage 7: Face the God who has sought you out.

When the heart is serene, we can turn to face the God who has sought us out. No longer fleeing, fearing, or erecting a facade, we are able to remain in his presence in peace. Finally, we realize that God is a person and that he desires to be a part of our life, that we have always been a part of his plan. Walls created by urges toward self-preservation and self-protection are gone, and we are free to gaze into God's eyes and to let him look into ours. There is nothing between us and God, our faces shining in the brightness of his face. As Paul put it: "All of us, with our unveiled faces like mirrors reflecting the glory of the Lord, are being transformed into the image that we reflect in brighter and brighter glory" (2 Cor 3:18 NJB).

We are transfigured; our lives become brighter and brighter with an authentic humanness revealing the glory of Christ. Christ Jesus imprints himself on us, on the deepest levels of our existence. The Word of God gives us form and configures us to himself. Jesus, the unique Way, Truth, and Life, transforms us into himself, laying complete hold to every aspect of our existence. As we turn away from this "present world" to the glory of Christ, we are shaped in Christ, according to his form. We are renewed until we are configured entirely to the archetype Christ, and we are a new creation (cf. 2 Cor 5.17; Gal 6.15). This transformation is not the result primarily of our own endeavors. It comes from permitting the actively shaping power of God in Christ to work in us. It is letting ourselves be renewed.

# Hold on to Hope

Blessed be God the Father of our Lord Jesus Christ,
who has blessed us with all the spiritual blessings of heaven
in Christ.
Before the world was made, he chose us, chose us in Christ,
to be holy and spotless, and to live through love in his
presence,
determining that we should become his adopted children,
through Jesus Christ
for his own kind purposes,
to make us praise the glory of his grace,
his free gift to us in the Beloved,
in whom, through his blood, we gain our freedom,
the forgiveness of our sins.
Such is the richness of the grace
which he has showered upon us
in all wisdom and insight.
He has let us know the mystery of his purpose,
the hidden plan he so kindly made in Christ from
the beginning

to act upon when the times had run their course to the end:
that he would bring everything together under Christ,
    as head,
everything in the heavens and everything on earth.
And it is in him that we were claimed as God's own,
chosen from the beginning,
under the predetermined plan of the one who guides
    all things
as he decides by his own will;
chosen to be,
for his greater glory,
the people who would put their hopes in Christ before
    he came.
Now you too, in him,
have heard the message of the truth and the good news
    of your salvation,
and have believed it;
and you too have been stamped with the seal of the
    Holy Spirit of the Promise,
the pledge of our inheritance
which brings freedom for those whom God has taken
    for his own,
to make his glory praised.

*(Eph 1:3–14 JB)*

BOOKS & MEDIA

A mission of the Daughters of St. Paul

As apostles of Jesus Christ, evangelizing today's world:

We are CALLED to holiness
by God's living Word and Eucharist.

We COMMUNICATE the Gospel message
through our lives and through all
available forms of media.

We SERVE the Church
by responding to the hopes and needs
of all people with the Word of God,
in the spirit of St. Paul.

For more information visit our website: www.pauline.org.

# BOOKS & MEDIA

The Daughters of St. Paul operate book and media centers at the following addresses. Visit, call or write the one nearest you today, or find us on the World Wide Web, www.pauline.org

**CALIFORNIA**

| | |
|---|---|
| 3908 Sepulveda Blvd, Culver City, CA 90230 | 310-397-8676 |
| 2640 Broadway Street, Redwood City, CA 94063 | 650-369-4230 |
| 5945 Balboa Avenue, San Diego, CA 92111 | 858-565-9181 |

**FLORIDA**

| | |
|---|---|
| 145 S.W. 107th Avenue, Miami, FL 33174 | 305-559-6715 |

**HAWAII**

| | |
|---|---|
| 1143 Bishop Street, Honolulu, HI 96813 | 808-521-2731 |
| Neighbor Islands call: | 866-521-2731 |

**ILLINOIS**

| | |
|---|---|
| 172 North Michigan Avenue, Chicago, IL 60601 | 312-346-4228 |

**LOUISIANA**

| | |
|---|---|
| 4403 Veterans Memorial Blvd, Metairie, LA 70006 | 504-887-7631 |

**MASSACHUSETTS**

| | |
|---|---|
| 885 Providence Hwy, Dedham, MA 02026 | 781-326-5385 |

**MISSOURI**

| | |
|---|---|
| 9804 Watson Road, St. Louis, MO 63126 | 314-965-3512 |

**NEW YORK**

| | |
|---|---|
| 64 W. 38th Street, New York, NY 10018 | 212-754-1110 |

**PENNSYLVANIA**

| | |
|---|---|
| Philadelphia—relocating | 215-969-5068 |

**SOUTH CAROLINA**

| | |
|---|---|
| 243 King Street, Charleston, SC 29401 | 843-577-0175 |

**VIRGINIA**

| | |
|---|---|
| 1025 King Street, Alexandria, VA 22314 | 703-549-3806 |

**CANADA**

| | |
|---|---|
| 3022 Dufferin Street, Toronto, ON M6B 3T5 | 416-781-9131 |

¡También somos su fuente para libros,
videos y música en español!